antonio carluccio's

SOUTHERN ITALIAN FEAST

antonio
carlu

CCIO'S
SOUTHERN
ITALIAN
FEAST

WITH FOOD PHOTOGRAPHS BY
PHILIP WEBB

BBC BOOKS

This book is published to accompany the television series *Antonio Carluccio's Southern Italian Feast,* which was produced by Bazal Productions for BBC Television.
Executive Producer: Peter Bazalgette
Production Manager: Susan King
Director: Caius Julyan

Published by BBC Books,
an imprint of BBC Worldwide Ltd,
Woodlands, 80 Wood Lane,
London W12 0TT

First published 1998
© Antonio Carluccio 1998
The moral right of the author
has been asserted

Food photography by Philip Webb
© 1998 BBC Worldwide Ltd.
All other photographs by Cassie Farrell, except page 5 by Steve Watkins, pages 12, 18 and 27 by Antonio Carluccio/Gennaro Contaldo and pages 35, 104 and 172 by Susan King.

ISBN 0 563 38393 3

Project Editor: Sally Potter
General Editor: Jane Middleton

Creative Director: Frank Phillips
Designer: Harry Green
Stylist: Helen Payne

Set in Baskerville and Futura
Printed and bound in Great Britain by Butler and Tanner Ltd, Frome
Colour separations by Radstock Reproductions Ltd, Midsomer Norton
Jacket printed by Lawrence Allen Ltd, Weston-super-Mare

Any of the speciality ingredients used in this book should be available from good Italian delicatessens. A wide range is stocked at:

Carluccio's
28a Neal Street
London WC2H 9PS
Tel: 0171-240 1487
Fax: 0171-497 1361

Details of other stockists of Carluccio's products may be obtained from this address. Carluccio's also runs a mail order service.

Some of the recipes in this book include wild mushrooms. Cooking and eating some species of wild mushroom can be dangerous. If you have any doubts at all about the species of fungus you have picked, do not eat it. Neither the publisher nor the author can accept any responsibility for the consequences of any mistaken identification of mushroom species.

I dedicate this book to my step-grandchildren,
Scott, Milton, Theo, Mo and Molly,
who give me the satisfaction of being
called Grandpa Cep.

To Jane

Cibita and love

Antonio Carluccio

ACKNOWLEDGEMENTS

My warmest thanks go to the following for having
contributed in one way or another to this book:
Arch. Mattia Antonio Aciti; Arch. Riccardo Dalisi;
Don Pippo Benedetto; Vivien Bowler;
Priscilla Carluccio; Carluccio's; Francesco Casertano;
Antonino Colonna; Gennaro Contaldo; my Aunt Dora;
Luciana Florio; Hotel Giordano, Ravello;
Hotel Su Gologone, Sardinia; Instituto Cavalcanti,
Accademia della Pizza, Napoli; Jane Middleton;
The Neal Street Restaurant; Caterina and
Antonio Palmeri; Pastificio Setaro; Donatella Limentani
Pavoncello; Helen Payne; Isabella Pezzolla;
Frank Phillips; Signor Pizzimenti; Sally Potter;
Liz Przybylski; Gherardo Scapinelli; Steve Watkins;
Philip Webb.

CONTENTS

'Chist'é o paese do' sole' says a popular

old Neapolitan song. Absolutely right –

this is the 'land of the sun'.

INTRODUCTION

The land of the sun is where I was fortunate enough to be born. My father was stationmaster in the village of Vietri Sul Mare on the splendid Amalfi coast, and originally came from Benevento in Campania. When I was three months old my family moved up to the North, where I grew up in another splendid area, the Monferrato. I feel particularly lucky to have had an multi-regional upbringing because it taught me, through the culinary genius of my mother, the basics of what was to become my professional passion, Italian food. Unlike most Italians, who are very parochial about food, my mother used to cook recipes from other regions regardless of where we happened to live. As a result, she developed a large repertoire of specialities, many from the South, which made the task of nourishing a family of six children less daunting even in wartime. Her talent for using very simple ingredients imaginatively meant that she fed us succulent and appetizing dishes which we always devoured with gusto, even if it was just cabbage.

Food is a very important part of life for Italians and they dedicate quite a large part of their income to it, convinced that it is a source of nourishment not only for the body but for the mind, too. You only have to observe an entire family eating together to see that food is an important catalyst for keeping the social spirit of a small community intact.

This passion for good food is shared by everyone in Italy, rich and poor alike. In the past, the poor had to rely on their ingenuity to create a varied and interesting diet out of limited resources. Known as *cucina povera*, the sort of dishes they ate are now being hailed as the classics of modern Italian cooking. Restaurants are rediscovering these dishes and putting them on their menus, using local ingredients cultivated by small producers who share their concern for quality.

Flower-covered hills of Sicily in spring

The currently fashionable Mediterranean diet, 'discovered' by American nutritionists, is nothing new in Italy, especially in the South where all those precious elements now considered essential for a well-balanced diet – olive oil, pasta, pulses, bread, fresh fruit, vegetables, fish, white meat and game – were used 2,000 years ago much as they are today.

Nevertheless, the Mediterranean diet has to be taken with a pinch of salt and, in my opinion, pepper too. The healthy label on these foods is well deserved but, in the quest for a healthy lifestyle, cooking ingredients are just part of the picture. In the South there are all the elements needed to live well. Food is so much more enjoyable if it is eaten in the appropriate surroundings and with convivial company. You are much more likely to enjoy a simple dish of fish and vegetables, followed by succulent ripe fruit and washed down with local wine, if you share it with friends under a pergola, with a blue sky above, the blue sea ahead and the hot sun beating down, than if you eat it alone in a small flat in a grey and polluted city.

A general enthusiasm for good food encourages the production of first-class ingredients. In Italy you can still buy quality ingredients from small shops or market stalls, which are keen to attract discerning customers by selling only the best. Supermarkets are finally gaining momentum in Italy, claiming to sell a wider variety of food than traditional outlets. Although I respect their efforts, I must say that the results are not always satisfactory. When goods become mass produced, quality is often the first casualty. What's more, supermarkets rarely employ staff with specialist knowledge who can draw customers' attention to the quality of what's on offer. And the temptations of seemingly unlimited choice often mean that shoppers throw caution and their better judgement to the winds, ending up with an enormous trolley piled high with superfluous items.

I am glad that at least in Italy, and especially in the South, small farmers still produce a cornucopia of wonderful vegetables and fruit, taking the utmost care to achieve the best produce, which still finds a place in small shops. The vendors know how to exhibit their merchandise invitingly and, above all, still offer customers that special personal chat, which often reveals a new way of cooking or preparing a certain food. The skill of the customer comes into play in trying to find out which are the best of the best, and going to some lenghts to stay loyal to them.

In Italy, laws enforced by local market authorities ensure that all foods on sale meet certain standards. However, I follow with some concern the movements of the EU legislators, who would like to regulate ways of making cheese, preserves and other goods, thus doing away with regional varieties. The day genuine artisan products, which have been made in the same way for centuries, become subject to this type of legislation is the day good food will cease to exist.

After filming throughout the South of Italy and visiting as many markets and shops as possible, I am glad to say that this point has not yet been reached. The enthusiasm of local people in helping me to portray the very best side of culinary Italy has been overwhelming. The entire crew benefited from genuine Southern hospitality, which made our task so much easier. It is my honour and privilege to present here what I believe to be the mother of all cuisines. Enjoy *Southern Italian Feast!*

ANTONIO CARLUCCIO

THE SOUTHERN ITALIAN LARDER

The culinary scene in the South is totally different from that of the North and the larder may look a little meagre in comparison. This is partly because of the very nature of the South – all that sun and almost year-round fresh fruit and vegetables – and partly because of the way of life. Most cooking ingredients are bought fresh on a daily basis, only occasionally ending up as leftovers for the next day.

Nevertheless, there are several staple ingredients that can be kept in stock at home, relatively safe from the torrid heat of summer. In winter some items are stored in that ideal natural fridge, the balcony. Southern Italians are very fond of their balcony, where in a netted box they keep anything from cheese and preserved

meats to *pomodorini* and salted anchovies – not to mention dishes such as *soffritto alla Napoletana* (see page 113), a base for sauces and stews which is made in large batches and then kept in a block (solidified by the cold) to be used a little at a time. The *dispensa*, or storecupboard, next to the kitchen usually combines a broom cupboard with the food storage rack. Some items, especially preserves and bottles of wine for special occasions, are kept in the cellar if there is one.

I have heard an anecdote about a peasant who many years ago was assigned a small flat on the outskirts of Naples, as part of a movement to house poor people in council properties. He filled up the bath with earth so he could cultivate fresh basil and parsley. When the social services queried his hygiene arrangements he replied that fresh herbs were much more useful! I hope this is only a story but, looked at from the point of view of someone used to living in the countryside without such sanitation, it makes a lot of sense.

Spaghetti dried traditionally

Sharing an authentic Sicilian shepherd's picnic

Between this Southern larder and the Northern one I wrote about in my book *Italian Feast*, the basic list of ingredients for good regional Italian food is complete. I hope you will have fun putting together your own Italian larder, and do bear in mind that if you see an irresistible item on offer you should buy it. It will later serve its purpose.

PASTA

A larder without pasta would not be a larder. Southern Italians always like to keep a few types of commercial dried pasta in stock for daily use, making their own egg pasta for special occasions. Of the 600 or so pasta shapes available, here are some of the most common dried varieties.

Spaghetti is probably the most versatile type of pasta. Each region produces its own version with slight variations, such as using a different method of extrusion – which results in a very smooth finish in the Neapolitan and Sicilian style and a slightly rough surface in the Pugliese spaghetti – or a different type of durum wheat semolina. Spaghetti goes with any type of sauce.

Lasagnoni, extra large sheets of pasta, and **brettelle** (meaning braces), sheets of pasta about 5 cm (2 in) wide, are used to make timbales and other baked pasta dishes.

Maccheroni is popular everywhere from Lazio to Sicily, and is served mostly with slow-cooked ragù sauces based on tomatoes with beef, lamb, pork or a mixture of these.

Linguine is a sort of flat spaghetti, oval rather than round, and is ideal for seafood sauces.

Pasta corta includes various short pasta shapes such as tubetti and ditali, which are particularly suitable for thick soups. The Neapolitans have a curious but thrifty habit of using a mixture of all the odds and ends of pasta left in the storecupboard, including the longer ones broken into pieces, to make an excellent *Pasta e Fagioli* (see page 72).

Orecchiette is a typical Pugliese pasta shaped like little ears, hence the name. It was traditionally made by hand but nowadays is more often commercially produced. Made from durum wheat semolina, it takes twice as long to cook as ordinary pasta and still remains *al dente*, or slightly chewy. Serve with vegetable sauces, especially broccoli.

Rigatoni, a short ribbed pasta, and **ziti**, long narrow tubes, are usually baked with lots of goodies to make timbales for grand occasions.

Gnocchetti sardi, also known as malloreddus, are very small, saffron-flavoured gnocchi exclusive to Sardinia. They are usually served with meat ragù or vegetable sauces.

FLOUR

Doppio zero (double zero, or 00) flour is a superfine soft wheat flour that is particularly suitable for making pasta, with or without eggs. *Tipo 0* (single zero) flour is often used for pizza and bread. The famous durum wheat semolina is a very coarse, creamy-yellow flour, also used for bread and in commercially manufactured pasta. Polenta flour is sometimes kept in the Southern larder but is not such a staple as in the North, and tends to be the white maize variety.

BREAD

The Southern Italians like to eat firmer, heavier bread than the rest of Italy.

Pane Pugliese, a huge, round loaf made of hard durum wheat, has good keeping qualities, which means it only need be bought weekly, although other types of bread are rigorously bought fresh each day. The Pugliese loaf is often used to make *bruschetta*.

Frisella is always kept at the ready in the larder. A round or oblong flat loaf, it is baked like ordinary bread, then thickly sliced and baked again to dry out so it keeps almost indefinitely. After being moistened with water, it is mixed with tomatoes, olive oil, garlic and basil or oregano to make *Panzanella* (see page 69), the most perfect snack, or used in various tomato-based soups or stuffing mixtures for baked vegetables.

Taralli are a must. They are small, ring-shaped biscuits made of durum wheat flour, olive oil and fennel seeds and baked until crisp. Like Northern grissini, they are eaten with *antipasti*.

Pane grattugiato, or dried breadcrumbs, are indispensable in the kitchen for dusting meat or vegetables before frying and also for stuffings or for thickening sauces.

TOMATOES

Absolutely essential in Southern Italian cooking, tomatoes are used daily in one way or another and are preserved in various ways so their flavour can be enjoyed all year round.

Pomodori pelati are peeled tomatoes, traditionally canned or bottled, mostly used in winter when fresh ones are not available. The best are preserved in Salerno, using San Marzano plum tomatoes which are excellent for sauces.

Polpa di pomodoro (tomato pulp or crushed tomatoes) consists of chunks of deseeded tomatoes in their own juice. It is suitable for any type of sauce.

Passata is a smoother version of *polpa*. Both *polpa* and *passata* are beginning to overtake the traditional peeled tomatoes in popularity.

Concentrato di pomodoro, or tomato paste, is always present in the larder. It is available in two forms: as double concentrate and as six-times concentrate, a very dark, thick paste known as *estratto*. Both are used as flavourings and to thicken tomato sauces. Now found mostly in Sicily, *estratto* was the first ever attempt to preserve tomatoes in Italy, in the 19th century when they were first processed commercially. To make it, tomato pulp is left in the sun and stirred a couple of times a day for a fortnight until all the water has evaporated. It is then mixed with salt, shaped into solid blocks and wrapped in basil leaves for extra flavour. I like it spread on a slice of toasted bread, rubbed with garlic and drizzled with extra virgin olive oil. Delicious!

Pomodori in bottiglia are made at home by quartering ripe San Marzano plum tomatoes, then pushing them into a bottle and sterilizing them. If you make a pasta sauce with these tomatoes, the full summer flavour comes back even in the depths of winter. Although they are mostly privately produced, you may find some in jars in very good Italian delicatessans, labelled as *filetti di pomodoro*.

Pomodori secchi, or sun-dried tomatoes, are prepared in August and September. Halved tomatoes are sprinkled with coarse salt and laid out on tables under the hot sun to dry. They are later rehydrated with water and vinegar to serve as delicious morsels for the *antipasto* or to flavour soups and sauces.

Families that can afford to do so – and judging by the number of red bunches hanging from balconies they seem to be many – buy *pomodorini*, very sweet, small tomatoes the size and shape of a cherry. Thanks to their tough skin they keep throughout the winter months.

Some families keep all these types of tomato in their larder, from which can be judged the position of honour and importance the tomato holds in Southern Italian cooking.

PRESERVED MEAT

Meat, mostly pork, is preserved partly by choice and partly through necessity in the South of Italy. However, although Southern Italians are extremely fond of pork and pork products, there are no huge industries for them in the South as there are in the North – for example in Emilia Romagna, where Parma ham and salami are produced. In the South, pork delicacies are either made privately, by the many people in rural areas who raise their own pigs, or are of artisan origin. This means the products tend to be of particularly high quality. The pigs are butchered in winter, and in private homes this represents a grand occasion, when friends are invited to feast on all the parts of the animal that are not suitable for preserving. It is quite usual for the entire village to participate in these celebrations, as has been the custom for centuries. Sometimes festivals known as *sagre* are held, which cover a larger area. In this case, however, little is provided *gratis* and profits go to fill the local community coffers. The main thing is that they are very jolly celebrations indeed, with food and wine enjoyed on a grand scale.

Below are the main salted and air-dried pork preserves used in cooking:

Guanciale consists of the cheek of the pig, a fatty, layered cut which is salt-cured and dried. It is used in sauces, soups and ragùs and is particularly popular in Lazio and Abruzzo.

Pancetta, from the belly of the pig, is the Italian version of streaky bacon and is widely used.

Lardo is a thick layer of pork fat, sometimes as much as 10 cm (4 in) deep. It is cut into small cubes and fried with onions and herbs to make a flavoursome base for all sorts of soups, sauces and meat ragùs.

All the following pork products are eaten as *antipasti* or snacks. These extremely tasty items have also found their way up to the North of Italy, where they were introduced by Southern immigrants and have won great popularity for their spicy flavour and high quality.

Prosciutto crudo, a type of cured ham, is the hind leg of the pig, which is salted and then air-dried for at least a year. The Southern version is totally different from the well-known Parma and San Daniele hams. It is usually saltier and is sometimes cured with *peperoncino* (chilli), a widely used spice.

Capocollo is part of the neck and shoulder of the pig, cut into large chunks, salted and spiced, then left in a skin to dry for at least four months and up to a year. It is eaten raw in thin slices. Particularly good versions are produced in Campania and Puglia, where it is sometimes smoked.

Soppressata is a type of sausage made from hand-cut cubes of lean pork and fat. These cubes are mixed with wine, garlic and flavourings, forced into a skin and pressed (hence the name *soppressata*), then air-dried for three months to a year and eaten raw. Its flavourings of fennel, chilli and spices make this sausage a very different product from its Northern counterpart. The Pugliese and Calabrese versions are exceptionally good.

Salsiccia is a 5 cm (2 in) thick intestine filled with minced pork and flavoured with salt, pepper, wine, chilli and sometimes fennel seeds. It can be eaten fresh but is usually air-dried for a few months and then thickly sliced and served with bread. The *salsiccia piccante napoletana* is a famous example, tied into a round shape, while the Calabrese version is highly spiced with lots of chilli.

Ciccioli, or *cicoli* as they are called in Naples and *sfrizzoli* in Rome, are the pieces left after pork fat has been melted to obtain *strutto* (see page 18). They are pressed and then cured with salt, pepper and bay leaves. *Ciccioli* can be eaten with bread or used in cooking, especially to make *pane con i ciccioli*, a highly flavoured bread. Needless to say, these pork scratchings still contain a lot of lard; they are extremely tasty but very naughty!

CHEESE

Cheesemaking is an ancient tradition in the South but was only relatively recently established in the North. Yet thanks to the North's wonderful green pastures and abundance of cow's milk mean that it has become a major industry there, while in the South and the islands, handicapped by the strong sun and lack of rain, it is still in the hands of small artisan companies. Sheep, goats and buffalo are raised, with only a few cows, resulting in a totally different range of cheeses. They tend to be rather pungent and are used locally both in cooking and for eating with bread.

Mozzarella is perhaps the most famous Southern cheese in the world, thanks to the popularity of the pizza. The international demand for it is so huge that the cow's milk version is now made all over Italy. The very best mozzarella is made with milk from buffaloes. These wonderful animals are reared almost exclusively for their precious milk and were first introduced in Italy by the Romans (who else?), who found an ideal habitat for them in Campania, Lazio and Puglia. Genuine fresh buffalo mozzarella is wonderful and should be eaten on the day it is made. The curd is heated in its own whey and then worked by hand until it is elastic enough to produce a stringy paste. This is then formed into balls, which should still exude a little milk when cut open. It is rather difficult to buy this type of mozzarella outside Italy because of the problem of transporting it. The next best thing is *mozzarella di bufala* sold in a sealed plastic bag containing some of the whey to keep it fresh and moist.

Mozzarella has hundreds of uses in cooking, such as on pizza, in calzone, or sliced and added to vegetable and pasta timbales. My favourite way of eating it is very simply, either accompanied by tomatoes and basil or just sprinkled with good olive oil, salt and pepper as an *antipasto*.

Scamorza and **provola** are made in a similar way to mozzarella but are hardened. Scamorza is sometimes sliced and grilled, while provola can be eaten as a table cheese or used in cooking.

Provolone, made in Campania and Sicily, is a huge cow's milk cheese with a layered structure like mozzarella. It is available as *dolce* (mild) and *piccante* (piquant). Both versions are used as table cheeses and in cooking.

Caciocavallo is similar to provolone but has a stronger flavour and firmer texture. Made of sheep's milk, it is a typical Sicilian cheese. It can be cut into cubes and grilled, added to vegetable stuffings, or grated for use instead of Parmesan.

Pecorino, the archetypal sheep's milk cheese, is made all over the region, from Lazio, where it is called pecorino romano, to Sardinia, where it is known as pecorino sardo. (The Sardinians have a tradition of eating pecorino when it is so old that maggots have developed inside – they call this *tasumarzu*. It is not a custom I would recommend.) Pecorino is available both fresh and aged. *Caciotta*, the fresh version, is eaten as a table cheese, while *stagionato*, the firmer, aged variety, can be grated as well. The intense, sweet taste of sheep's milk makes pecorino indispensable in many Southern dishes. Curiously, however, although pecorino is produced in the South, it is now very popular in the North, while it is the other way round for Parmesan. In fact it is considered rather posh in the South to use grated Parmesan on pasta and vegetables. Perhaps the unification of Italy, which took place only about 130 years ago, is still in progress.

Ricotta, a soft, low-fat cheese, is really a by-product of cheesemaking, since it is made from the whey that has separated from the curd. Any type of milk is suitable but in the South it tends to be sheep's or goat's milk. Ricotta, which has to

Tasumarzu is a rotten cheese crawling with maggots – a Sardinian speciality!

be eaten very fresh, can be used in hundreds of dishes, both savoury and sweet, and is particularly popular as a filling for calzoni and tarts. In Sicily it is used to make *cassata*, to stuff *Cannoli alla Siciliana* (see page 174) or simply eaten with sugar.

Ricotta salata is an aged salted cheese used mostly in Puglia, where it is grated over savoury dishes. It is quite hard and grey in colour and gives a distinctive tangy flavour to food.

OILS AND FATS

Extra virgin olive oil is mostly produced in Puglia, Campania, Calabria and Sicily and is obtained by cold pressing freshly picked olives. The finest of all oils, it tends to be used as a flavouring for salads and soups rather than in cooking. Every family keeps it as an essential storecupboard item. A simple olive oil is also kept for frying and for general cooking.

Sunflower, **corn** and **groundnut oils** are also used for frying. Besides being cheaper than olive oil, they can safely be heated to a higher temperature.

Strutto, or *sugna* as it is called in dialect, is pork fat that has been rendered and then left to cool so that it solidifies. In the past pork fat was a cheap and plentiful medium for frying and baking. In these more health-conscious times, its use is restricted to a few dishes where its flavour is considered essential.

Butter is used primarily as a flavouring ingredient, reserved for certain types of pastry, some pasta sauces and for frying fish. It is a newly acquired taste in the South, which arose from trying to reproduce North Italian dishes.

PULSES AND GRAINS

Both fresh and dried pulses are very popular throughout the South.

Cannellini beans can be found in any decent larder, usually dried but sometimes canned for immediate use. They come in handy for *pasta e fagioli* or for making into wholesome vegetable dishes, salads, stews and, naturally, minestrone.

Borlotti beans are used in the same way as cannellini.

Broad beans are very popular fresh in season but in the larder you will find some *fave secche* for winter – dried broad beans which are either turned into soups or puréed and served with olive oil and wild chicory to make the Pugliese dish *'ncapriata* (see page 150).

Chickpeas are another favourite. They are used mainly for soups and *pasta e ceci* but also in stews, salads and as an accompaniment to pork dishes. Chickpea flour is widely used in Sicily to make *panelle*, a type of fritter that is served in bread.

Lentils are very popular in the South. In Rome there is a New Year's Eve tradition of eating them with *zampone* (pig's trotters). Every Southern region has different dishes for them but they tend to be stewed or made into soups. They are exceptionally good cooked with borage, Campanian-style (see page 68).

Rice is not really a Southern speciality, although some rice dishes are eaten, including a seafood risotto that is more like a warm rice and seafood salad. In Lazio, and especially in Rome, rice timbales are made. Otherwise rice is used for stuffing tomatoes and peppers, to make the famous Sicilian *Arancini* (see page 91) and in soups. It can also be eaten plain, with just a little butter or olive oil. The most common variety of rice in the South is arborio, although in Sardinia a longish rice similar to patna is cultivated.

Durum wheat grain, or *grano*, is used mainly in Naples, where it is soaked and cooked in milk to make *pastiera di grano*, a famous sweet tart for Easter. Durum wheat is also made into a soup with beans and served as a side dish.

WINE VINEGAR

Red wine vinegar is the most common in Southern Italy and many families make their own. It is used mostly for vegetable preserves, which are then served as an *antipasto*, and for salad dressings and marinades. In Lazio they have a curious use for vinegar – it is sprinkled over fresh strawberries with sugar.

ANCHOVIES, TUNA AND BOTTARGA

These all play an important role in Southern Italian cooking. Everyone keeps anchovies in the larder – if not the salted variety, which are the most flavoursome, then at least in oil. They are produced in Calabria, Sicily and Sardinia.

Tuna is canned mostly in oil and is another convenient staple for salads, vegetable stuffings and sauces. One delicacy that not everyone can afford is *mosciame di tonno* – air-dried and salted fillet of tuna, which is eaten thinly sliced with oil and lemon as an *antipasto* or snack.

Equally precious is bottarga, the salted and air-dried roe of tuna or mullet, very much appreciated in Sicily, Calabria and especially Sardinia. This very fine food is eaten in slices with olive oil and lemon juice, or grated over pasta to impart a pungent but delicious fishy flavour.

FLAVOURINGS AND SPICES

Sometimes flavourings and spices are heavily used in countries where the local food is rather dull, in order to improve the taste. This is certainly not the case in Southern Italy, where they add an extra dimension to food that is already excellent, creating a wider variety of dishes.

Garlic and onions are used in sauces, roasts,

salads, marinades and stuffings. They are simply indispensable in the local cuisine and every family always keeps both in the larder.

Salt and pepper are culinary essentials. Salt not only brings out the flavour of food but is also used for preserving and as a thick crust in which to bake fish. There are two types of salt, *sale fine* and *sale grosso*, or coarse sea salt, which is produced in the town of Trapani in Sicily. Pepper is mostly black and is either freshly ground or added whole to broths and stock. It is also used to make salami.

Peperoncino, or dried chilli, is called *diavulillo* (little devil) in many places because of its ferociously hot power. It is cultivated throughout the South and used mostly dried. Every family keeps some beautifully arranged plaits or bunches hanging in the kitchen or on the balcony.

Fennel seeds are added to various dishes, breads and even sausages for their distinctive flavour. Southerners also love fresh fennel bulbs, which they even eat raw like fruit, and *finocchio selvatico*, or wild fennel (also called *finocchietto*), which features mainly in Sicilian cooking.

Capers are another old favourite in the South and are the buds of a plant, picked before blossoming into a splendid flower. They are available either salted, in brine or in vinegar, although connoisseurs prefer the salted variety, which have to be soaked in water before use to get rid of excess salt. Their distinctive taste is so strong that usually only a few are needed to flavour sauces and salads or as a garnish. The best capers come from the small Sicilian islands of Pantelleria and Lipari. If you find some salted ones in an Italian market during your holiday,

buy them in quantity because they keep for a couple of years.

Olives are a precious fruit, essential to all sorts of dishes, and in the land of the olive they are offered to the buyer in an infinite variety of forms. Southern Italians love to eat little snacks or *antipasti* containing black or green olives that have been 'improved' by mixing them with fennel seeds, garlic and chilli or even baking them in the oven, where they become dry and concentrated in flavour. Salads, pasta sauces, stews and roasts often contain olives.

Sometimes olives can be one of just a few items for a meal, as I found out when sharing a shepherd's lunch in Sicily. I have always been curious to know what a shepherd eats in the fields away from home, and I was not too surprised when Gaspare Campo produced home-made Sicilian durum wheat bread, which remains fresh and moist for several days, a slab of home-made pecorino cheese and some ricotta, freshly made that morning. What did surprise me, however, was the relatively sophisticated accompaniments – tomatoes, some fresh broad beans in their pods to eat with the cheese, an onion and some olives – which all combined to make a nourishing meal *al fresco*. My contribution of a Sicilian salami and a bottle of wine was welcome but wine is not customary. Because of the heat, water is more likely to be drunk to quench the thirst.

HERBS

Fresh herbs are the soul of Italian cooking. Used judiciously they can lift the taste of the simplest ingredients.

Parsley, **basil**, **sage**, **bay** and **rosemary** are the most common fresh herbs in the South, and the last two are also used dried.

Mint is also popular, especially in Lazio and Campania, where it makes an interesting addition to meat, fish and vegetables. The Romans like *nepetella*, a small-leaf variety of mint which is also used in Tuscany, Umbria and Abruzzo but not in the deep South.

Oregano is the one herb that is more often used dried than fresh because of its concentrated, minty wild flavour. Everyone keeps oregano in the larder. It is widely used in the South of Italy, as it is throughout the Mediterranean, to flavour pizza, tomato sauces – especially *pizzaiola* sauce – and above all for salads and with *frisella* (see page 14).

NUTS AND DRIED FRUIT

The use of nuts in cooking is widespread in the South, where they are added to sauces, stews and meat dishes, besides being a natural component of breads, cakes and desserts. Their presence is a reminder of the Arab influence on the area, especially in Sicily.

Pine kernels are small, longish white seeds from the cones of the umbrella pine, which grows along the Southern coastline. They are commonly used in salads, meat and vegetable stuffings, biscuits and cakes.

Hazelnuts are almost exclusively used in biscuits and cakes or eaten like fruit. The best ones come from Campania, and especially from Avellino, a town whose name comes from the Latin word for hazelnut, *avellana*.

Almonds are eaten more than any other nut in the South. The almond tree, which resembles a peach tree, is cultivated in Puglia, Calabria, Campania, Sardinia and especially in Sicily, where almonds are mostly turned into marzipan to make rich sweets such as *cassata* and various biscuits similar to amaretti.

Walnuts are cultivated mostly in the South, and the very best ones come from the area around Sorrento. Green walnuts that are still soft inside are macerated in pure alcohol, sugar and spices for 40 days to make a powerful liqueur called *nocino*. Dried walnuts, eaten in winter and especially at Christmas time, are sometimes covered with bitter chocolate to make an irresistible nibble.

Raisins are another example of the Arab influence on Southern cooking, especially the Sicilian *zibibbo* raisins from the grapes of the same name. They are added to vegetable stews such as *caponata*, meat sauces and stuffings, and, of course, biscuits and cakes.

Cedro is a type of candied peel made from the huge lemons that grow in Calabria and Sicily. The peel is candied with sugar and green colouring, which gives it an exotic flavour and appearance. Cut into small cubes, it is used in ricotta desserts, *cannoli* and many other Southern sweets. Ordinary lemon and orange peel are also candied and used in the same way.

Zucca is another candied item, made from extra-long courgettes which are cut lengthways into strips. It is used mostly in Sicily for making *cassata*.

appetizers

The *antipasto* – from the Latin *ante pastum*, meaning before the main meal – has the task of stimulating the palate and preparing the stomach for the dishes to follow. For major celebrations such as weddings, christenings, Christmas and Easter there can easily be as many as 12 *antipasti*. The custom of offering a wide choice of little dishes for the *antipasto* is a Northern one but it has recently taken the South by storm. Previously a Southern *antipasto* consisted of a few slices of salami or ham accompanied by some *sott'aceti* (pickles) and bread, just to stimulate the stomach juices. The irresistible variety and quality of the *antipasto* in the North can pose a real conundrum about whether to eat only *antipasto* or move on to the next course. Now that the South has taken to the *antipasto* so enthusiastically, diners there are faced with the same dilemma. Given the unparalleled choice of fresh produce and modern creativity of chefs, today's list of Southern *antipasti* is more than a match for the Northern one.

Perfectly in tune with modern preferences, the *antipasto* represents a lighter way of eating for health-conscious diners. Because it is based on imaginatively cooked vegetables it satisfies the body and the soul without expanding the figure. In Southern Italian restaurants you usually don't even need to order – as soon as you sit down you will be offered a selection of *antipasto*. These vary from place to place but often an array of roasted or grilled vegetables in oil, sliced ricotta, mozzarella, olives, artichokes, peppers, slices of *soppressata* (a very good salami), seafood salad, baked mussels, anchovies in oil and herbs, baked marinated sardines and other items is brought to your table, together with crisp *taralli* and a bottle of local wine. Incidentally, dishes like these are often eaten as little snacks between meals. A very pleasant way of life!

Previous pages: Selection of *antipasti*: (clockwise from top left) *Rotoli di Pomodori Secchi* (page 25); green olives; *frisella* with tomatoes and basil; *Mozzarella Con Olio d'Oliva* (page 33); *taralli*; *Buttarica al Limone* (page 34); salami; black olives

ROTOLI DI POMODORI SECCHI
Rolled Sun-dried Tomatoes

MAKES 20

20 large sun-dried tomatoes (leave the halves of each tomato attached)

1 teaspoon dried oregano

4 tablespoons extra virgin olive oil

1 tablespoon salted capers, soaked in water for 10 minutes, then drained

1 tablespoon mint leaves

20 anchovy fillets in oil

Choose very large sun-dried tomatoes for this dish in order to roll them up with the filling. Sun-dried tomatoes can be used in various ways or enjoyed plain as a snack. However, they are quite salty so it is best to soak them before use in two parts vinegar to one part water for an hour or so, then drain and pat dry. They can then be flavoured with basil, oregano, garlic or chilli and covered with olive oil to be eaten later on. Alternatively, try this recipe.

METHOD

Desalt and soften the sun-dried tomatoes as described above. Sprinkle them with the oregano and olive oil. Open out the tomato halves and place a few capers, mint leaves and an anchovy fillet in each tomato. Roll up to enclose the filling. Spear each roll with a cocktail stick to serve, if liked.

INVOLTINI DI MELANZANE
Aubergine Rolls

SERVES 4

12 long slices of aubergine, 5 mm (¼ in) thick

Olive oil for frying

10 tablespoons fresh breadcrumbs, lightly toasted

12 olives, pitted and coarsely chopped

6 tablespoons coarsely grated pecorino cheese

1 tomato, very finely chopped

12 basil leaves

Salt and freshly ground black pepper

Aubergines are greatly enjoyed in Puglia, Calabria, Sicily and Basilicata, and naturally many recipes for them have developed. This is one of the simplest.

METHOD

Preheat the oven to 200°C, 400°F, Gas Mark 6.

Cook the aubergine slices in boiling salted water for 2 minutes, then drain and pat dry. Heat some oil in a large frying pan and fry the aubergine slices until brown on both sides. Lay the slices out on a work surface.

Mix together the toasted breadcrumbs, olives, half the pecorino cheese and the tomato, then season to taste with salt and pepper. Spread the mixture over the aubergine slices, place a basil leaf on top of each one and roll up, securing the rolls with a wooden cocktail stick. Place the rolls on a baking tray, sprinkle the rest of the pecorino cheese over them and bake for 10 minutes. They can be eaten hot or cold.

FUNGHI RIPIENI
Stuffed Mushrooms

12 open-cap mushrooms,
about 4 cm (1½ in) in
diameter

5 tablespoons fresh
breadcrumbs

½ garlic clove, very finely
chopped

4 tablespoons freshly grated
Parmesan cheese

2 eggs

1 tablespoon chopped fresh
marjoram

2 tablespoons dried
breadcrumbs

4 tablespoons olive oil

Salt and freshly ground black
pepper

Mushrooms are a much-loved seasonal speciality all over Italy, including the South. Recently the cultivated mushroom has been gaining popularity, especially when composing a decent selection of antipasti.

METHOD

Preheat the oven to 220°C, 425°F, Gas Mark 7.

Remove and discard the mushroom stalks. Mix together the fresh breadcrumbs, garlic, cheese, eggs, marjoram and salt and pepper and use to stuff the mushroom caps. Place the mushrooms stuffed-side up on an oiled baking tray. Sprinkle with the dried breadcrumbs and drizzle with the olive oil. Bake for 15 minutes, until the mushrooms are heated through and the filling is lightly browned.

Fruits of a day's mushroom picking:
Caesar's mushrooms and *porcini*

PEPERONI MANDORLATI
Almond Peppers

SERVES 4

4 tablespoons olive oil

2 yellow peppers, cut into strips

2 red peppers, cut into strips

2 tablespoons white wine vinegar

1 teaspoon sugar

40 g (1½ oz) raisins

40 g (1½ oz) split almonds

150 g (5 oz) *polpa di pomodoro* (see page 15)

Salt and freshly ground black pepper

This is one of many ways of preparing peppers in Sicily, where they are also served raw, roasted, sautéed and even air-dried.

METHOD

Heat the olive oil in a large pan and add the peppers. Fry on a gentle heat for about 10 minutes, stirring from time to time, until softened. Then add all the remaining ingredients and cook for a further 10 minutes. Season to taste. Serve hot, warm or cold.

ZUCCHINI E MELANZANE ALLA SCAPECE
Fried and Marinated Courgettes and Aubergines

SERVES 4

2 aubergines, cut into slices 5 mm (¼ in) thick

Olive oil for shallow-frying

4 courgettes, cut into slices 5 mm (¼ in) thick

1 bunch of mint, roughly chopped

4 tablespoons olive oil

1 tablespoon white wine vinegar

1 garlic clove, coarsely chopped

Salt

In the South, and particularly in Campania and Puglia, antipasti *are almost always served with some pickled vegetables such as* giardiniera *or some fried and marinated vegetables such as these courgettes and aubergines. They make a delicious snack or accompaniment to cold roast meat.*

METHOD

Blanch the aubergine slices in boiling salted water for 1 minute, then drain and pat dry (this prevents them absorbing too much oil when they are fried). Heat some oil in a large frying pan and fry the aubergines and courgettes in batches until brown on each side. Put them in a dish, sprinkle with salt, then add the mint, olive oil, vinegar and garlic. Mix well and leave to marinate for at least 2 hours.

Following pages (from left): *Peperoni Mandorlati* (page 28); *Zucchini e Melanzane alla Scapece* (above)

INVOLTINI DI PEPERONI ARROSTITI
Roasted Pepper Rolls

MAKES 12

4 very large red or yellow peppers

5 tablespoons fresh breadcrumbs

2 tablespoons finely chopped green olives

1 tablespoon salted capers, soaked in water for 10 minutes, then drained and finely chopped

½ garlic clove, finely chopped

3 tablespoons extra virgin olive oil, plus extra for brushing

6 anchovy fillets, finely chopped

2 tablespoons finely chopped fresh parsley

Salt and freshly ground black pepper

I very much like the idea of a surprise in an involtino. *A piece of meat, fish or vegetable is rolled around a stuffing mixture and then cooked. Here the peppers are cooked twice: first they are roasted to make them pliable and give them a charcoal flavour, then they are rolled up with the filling and baked. The result is very scrumptious indeed.*

METHOD

Preheat the oven to 200°C, 400°F, Gas Mark 6.

Roast the peppers on a charcoal grill (or under a very hot oven grill) until black and blistered on all sides, turning them as necessary. Leave to cool, then peel off the skin and cut each pepper lengthways into 3. Discard the seeds.

Mix together all the remaining ingredients. Divide the mixture equally between the pepper strips and roll them up, securing each one with a wooden cocktail stick. Place the pepper rolls on an oiled baking tray and brush with oil, then bake for 10–12 minutes. Serve hot or cold.

MOZZARELLA O BURRATA CON OLIO D'OLIVA
Mozzarella with Olive Oil

SERVES 4

**2 very fresh buffalo
mozzarella, cut into slices
1 cm (½ in) thick**

**3 tablespoons extra virgin
olive oil**

**Salt and freshly ground black
pepper**

Mozzarella cheese is so versatile that, together with Parmesan, it virtually symbolizes dairy Italy. Besides being used in many cooked dishes, it is eaten both as an antipasto *and after a meal as the cheese course. The best is made with buffalo's milk, and comes from the South. One delicious variation of mozzarella is* burrata, *from Puglia, which has a strong, elastic outer skin containing a mixture of cream and soft filaments of cheese. While mozzarella keeps for a few days,* burrata *should be eaten immediately. This is why it is almost impossible to find outside Italy. Ideally* burrata *should be used in this recipe but top-quality buffalo mozzarella makes an excellent substitute.*

METHOD

Arrange the mozzarella slices on a plate. Drizzle with the olive oil and season with salt and pepper. Serve with taralli or grissini. You could add a few slices of tomato and some basil leaves to make the well-known dish *insalata caprese.*

BUTTARICA AL LIMONE
Bottarga with lemon

SERVES 4

200 g (7 oz) tuna bottarga, thinly sliced

Juice of 1 lemon

4 tablespoons olive oil

Freshly ground black pepper

Although bottarga is typical of both Sardinia and Sicily, it seems to have had Greek origins. Salting and drying fish – or in this case its roe – is an ancient method of preserving. Bottarga, particularly tuna bottarga, commands very high prices but nevertheless it is enjoyed by the rich and, in small quantities, by the less fortunate. Here it is served with a simple dressing but it can also be eaten with scrambled eggs or grated over pasta like Parmesan.

METHOD

Arrange the bottarga slices on serving plates. Drizzle with the lemon juice and olive oil and sprinkle with freshly ground black pepper. Serve with bread – I like it with buttered crusty bread.

Anchovies are preserved in salt in these glazed terracotta pots for *antipasti*

COZZE ALLA TARANTINA
Mussels Taranto-style

SERVES 4, OR MORE AS
PART OF AN *ANTIPASTO*

1 kg (2¼ lb) mussels

50 g (2 oz) *Aglio e Muddica*
(see page 59)

Olive oil for drizzling

4 tablespoons tomato juice

4 tablespoons dry white wine

High-quality mussels are cultivated in Taranto, the large Italian port in the Gulf of Taranto in Puglia. The flavour of these mussels is so good that you need add very few ingredients to make a great dish. Mussels are cooked in this way in other regions, too, where they are known as cozze gratinate. They can be eaten hot or cold and are delicious.

METHOD

Preheat the oven to 200°C, 400°F, Gas Mark 6.

Scrub the mussels thoroughly under cold running water, pulling out the beards and discarding any open mussels that do not close when tapped on a work surface. Put the mussels in a large pan with 2 tablespoons of water. Cover and cook over a medium-high heat for 3–4 minutes, shaking the pan occasionally, until all the shells are open (discard any that remain closed).

Remove the top half of the shell from each mussel. Arrange the mussels in tightly packed rows on a baking tray and cover with the breadcrumb mixture. Drizzle with olive oil and bake for 8 minutes. Pour the tomato juice over the mussels and bake for a further 10 minutes. Pour over the white wine and bake for another 2 minutes.

FRUTTI DI MARE SALTATI
Mixed Shellfish

SERVES 4

2 kg (4½ lb) mixed shellfish,
  such as clams, prawns, sea
  dates and sea truffles

6 tablespoons olive oil

6 tablespoons dry white wine

2 tablespoons finely chopped
  fresh parsley

Freshly ground black pepper

Lemon wedges, to serve

This antipasto *is served in just about every coastal restaurant in Italy, where the local seafood is very fresh indeed. The shellfish are cooked just long enough to open and release their juices into the pan, giving this dish a real flavour of the sea. Combined with the oil and wine, the juice is so delicious that you will want to mop it all up from your plate with a piece of bread.*

Sea dates and sea truffles are considered real delicacies in Italy but are hard to find elsewhere. Sea dates actually look like dates and are related to mussels, while sea truffles are similar to clams. Other shellfish could be used, such as scallops and mussels.

METHOD

Scrub the molluscs under cold running water, discarding any open ones that don't close when tapped on a work surface. Heat the oil in a large pan and add all the shellfish. Pour in the wine and cover the pan. Cook over a medium-high heat for a few minutes, shaking the pan from time to time, until all the mollusc shells are open and the prawns are dark pink. Stir in the parsley and abundant black pepper, then serve immediately with lemon wedges.

Following pages:

Frutti di Mare Saltati (above)

INSALATA DI CICERIELLI
Salad of Elvers

SERVES 4

500 g (1 lb 2 oz) freshly caught baby sand eels

120 ml (4 fl oz) extra virgin olive oil

Juice of 2 lemons

3 tablespoons chopped fresh parsley

300 g (11 oz) smoked swordfish, very thinly sliced

Salt and freshly ground black pepper

Various newborn fish are offered from time to time in the famous Vucceria market of Palermo. They may be little anchovies or small sand eels, whichever are available on the day. These small fish are so delicate that they hardly require cooking; in fact some connoisseurs eat them raw, dressed with lemon juice and olive oil.

METHOD

Wash the eels well, making sure they are free of all impurities. Then blanch in a large pan of lightly salted boiling water for 15 seconds or a little longer, depending on size; they should become slightly paler. Drain and put in a bowl. Dress with the olive oil, lemon juice, parsley and some salt and pepper. Arrange 3 or 4 slices of swordfish on each serving plate and spoon a small pile of the dressed eels in the centre.

FRITTELLE DI CICERIELLI
Elver Fritters

MAKES 20

500 g (1 lb 2 oz) freshly caught baby sand eels

3 tablespoons dried breadcrumbs

3 eggs, beaten

1 tablespoon very finely chopped fresh parsley

Good olive oil for shallow-frying

Salt and freshly ground black pepper

Lemon wedges, to serve

Besides serving elvers (baby eels) as a salad, another way of eating them is as fritters. They make an excellent antipasto *and are also good served with drinks. If you cannot get elvers, newborn anchovies or even prawns can be used instead.*

METHOD

Wash the eels thoroughly, then drain well. Put them in a bowl with the breadcrumbs, eggs, parsley and some salt and pepper and mix together.

Heat plenty of olive oil in a frying pan. When it is very hot, add spoonfuls of the mixture and shallow-fry for only a couple of minutes, until crisp on both sides. Repeat until all the mixture is finished. Serve immediately, with lemon wedges.

PRIMI
first courses

After the *antipasto* it is time for *il primo*, the first course. In Southern Italy this is the most popular part of the meal because it offers a choice of pasta in all sorts of guises, plus soups made with vegetables or pulses, vegetables cooked with spices or herbs and, depending on the season, pasta salads.

In the past the *primo* was often the only course eaten by poor people – pasta accompanied by salad and followed by a little fresh fruit. Today many people eat like this through choice rather than economic necessity, although happily everyone can now afford meat and fish as well as vegetables and pasta.

In Lazio spaghetti and bucatini are the most popular pasta shapes, eaten with *guanciale* (see page 16) and eggs, as in *Spaghetti alla Carbonara* (see page 60) and *Bucatini Aglio e Muddica* (see page 59). Two very different Southern regions – Campania, or more specifically the area around Naples, and Puglia – have given the world some of the simplest and most popular pasta recipes. They are always made with good commercial dried pasta rather than the fresh egg pasta that is typical of Northern regions such as Emilia Romagna. Fresh pasta is made in the South, too, but traditionally does not include eggs. Fusilli, for example, a typically Campanian pasta, is made of flour and water only and shaped by turning small pieces of the dough around a kneading iron. It makes an excellent *primo* served with a tomato sauce or meat ragù. Spaghetti, which in Campania is called vermicelli (little worms), and linguine are possibly the most popular first courses. Served with simple sauces of tomatoes and basil or seafood such as clams and mussels, combined with the local olive oil and fresh, fragrant herbs, they are elevated to a superior experience for the tastebuds.

Orecchiette, a firm, chewy pasta from Puglia, is usually dressed with vegetables

Previous pages: *Culurzones* (page 54)

such as broccoli, the fantastic local olive oil, and seasoned with garlic and chilli. Cavatelli is similar to orecchiette but is mostly served with a heavy tomato sauce or seafood – see *Cavatelli con le Cozze* on page 49.

Pasta-based first courses are equally popular in Calabria and Sicily, where they are served uncompromisingly with lots of spices. Very often, salted anchovies are used as a flavouring, as they have been since ancient Roman times. *Pasta con le sarde* is an exceptionally good dish, made with the freshest of sardines and *finocchietto* (wild fennel). Sardinia has developed its own pasta shapes, the most popular of which are *gnocchetti sardi* (see page 64), usually served with a lamb or beef ragù, and *Culurzones* (see page 54), a type of home-made ravioli.

Rice is seldom served in the South. *Arancini*, deep-fried rice croquettes, are a speciality of Sicily. A seafood risotto is made but is nothing like the creamy risotto of the North. A Roman timbale of rice filled with porcini mushrooms and chicken giblets (see page 62) is excellent.

One of the most curious first courses, eaten in most Southern regions, is *Panzanella* (see page 69), a salad made of *frisella* (twice-baked bread) or stale leftover bread soaked in water and mixed with tomatoes, good olive oil and basil. It looks like chicken feed but tastes delicious.

Soup is also offered as a *primo*, and may be made of fish, vegetables or meat. *Pasta e Fagioli* (see page 72) is a hearty pasta and bean soup, while minestrone is a thick vegetable soup made throughout the South. *Pasta in brodo*, pasta cooked in a good chicken stock, is the lightest of the soups.

Gnocchi are dumplings made with flour and mashed potatoes and are very common throughout the South. In Naples, where they are usually dressed with a fresh tomato and basil sauce, they are called *strangolaprieviti*, meaning priest choker – a reference perhaps to the alleged greediness of the priesthood and their habit of cramming down their food! The gnocchi of Rome are completely different – a thick paste of semolina, milk and eggs, dotted with butter and sprinkled with Parmesan cheese, then baked in the oven. Inspired by the *panelle* (chickpea fritters) of Palermo and the gnocchi of Rome, I invented gnocchi made with chickpea flour (see page 65).

Last but not least, coarse semolina is used in the South to make couscous. Originally a North African dish, this has been adopted in Sicily, specifically in the town of Trapani, where it is served with a light fish stew.

In the land of the sun (the temple at Segesta, Sicily)

CANNOLICCHI CON FRITTELLA
Pasta with Artichokes, Broad Beans and Peas

SERVES 4

6 tablespoons extra virgin olive oil

200 g (7 oz) onions, finely sliced

8 tender artichoke hearts

200 g (7 oz) young peas (shelled weight)

200 g (7 oz) young broad beans (shelled weight)

2 tablespoons coarsely chopped fresh parsley

400 g (14 oz) cannolicchi (long macaroni) or macaroni

Salt and freshly ground black pepper

Freshly grated Parmesan cheese, to serve

A typical Sicilian pasta dish combining an unusual pasta shape with an interesting sauce. Frittella, *the pride of Palermo, can be made in different ways but always uses the best springtime produce such as fresh peas, broad beans and artichokes.*

METHOD

Heat the olive oil in a pan, add the onions and fry gently until softened. Meanwhile, prepare the artichokes: cut the top third off each one and discard the tough outer leaves until you reach the tender heart. Peel the stems, then cut the artichokes into quarters, scraping away the chokes if they are large. Add the artichokes, peas, broad beans and a glass of water to the pan. Cover and cook for 15 minutes, stirring from time to time and adding a little more water if the mixture becomes dry. Add the parsley and some seasoning and cook for a further 5 minutes, until the vegetables are tender.

Cook the pasta in plenty of boiling salted water until *al dente*. Drain, reserving a little of the cooking water. Add the pasta and reserved cooking water to the vegetables and mix well. Serve with grated Parmesan cheese.

ORECCHIETTE CON BROCCOLI E PROSCIUTTO
Orecchiette with Broccoli and Ham

SERVES 4

6 tablespoons olive oil

50 g (2 oz) prosciutto, cut into small cubes

1 garlic clove, finely chopped

½ chilli, finely chopped

6 small cherry tomatoes, quartered

200 g (7 oz) broccoli florets

2 tablespoons finely chopped fresh parsley

400 g (14 oz) orecchiette

40 g (1½ oz) pecorino cheese, grated (optional)

Salt and freshly ground black pepper

The purists of Puglian cuisine will be horrified at my audacity in adding ham to the classic dish orecchiette con cime di rape *and substituting broccoli for turnip tops. However, I find it an extremely good combination and still in keeping with the region.*

METHOD

Heat the oil in a pan, add the prosciutto and fry for a few minutes. Add the garlic, chilli and tomatoes and fry briefly, then stir in the broccoli florets and a little water. Cover the pan and cook gently until the broccoli is tender, then stir in the parsley.

Meanwhile, cook the pasta in a large pan of lightly salted boiling water for 12–15 minutes, until *al dente*. Drain and add to the sauce. Mix well and season with salt and pepper. Serve with the pecorino cheese if desired.

CAVATELLI CON LE COZZE
Cavatelli with Mussels

SERVES 4

1 kg (2¼ lb) mussels

6 tablespoons extra virgin
olive oil, plus extra to serve

1 garlic clove, finely chopped

1 small chilli, finely diced

300 g (11 oz) cherry
tomatoes

1 small bunch of flat-leaf
parsley, finely chopped

400 g (14 oz) cavatelli pasta

Salt and freshly ground black
pepper

A speciality of Puglia and particularly of Bari, where cavatelli are still hand-made for special occasions from hard durum wheat semolina flour and water. You can buy high-quality commercially manufactured cavatelli in good delicatessens. As it is quite soupy, this pasta dish may be eaten with a spoon.

METHOD

Scrub the mussels thoroughly under cold running water, pulling out the beards and discarding any open mussels that do not close when tapped on a work surface. Put the mussels in a large pan with 2 tablespoons of water, cover and cook over a medium-high heat for 3–4 minutes, shaking the pan occasionally, until all the shells are open (discard any that remain closed). Remove the shells from half the mussels. Strain the cooking juices through a very fine sieve and reserve.

Heat the oil in a frying pan, add the garlic and chilli and fry gently until the garlic is softened but not browned. Cut some of the cherry tomatoes in half. Add the halved and the whole tomatoes to the pan and fry until softened. Add the mussels, their cooking juices and the parsley and heat through gently. Season with salt and pepper to taste.

Meanwhile, cook the pasta in a large pan of lightly salted boiling water until *al dente*. Drain and stir into the mussel sauce. I like to pour a stream of extra virgin olive oil on to each portion for extra flavour.

LINGUINE DI PORTO BADISCO (CON I RICCI)
Linguine with Sea Urchins

SERVES 4

The roe of 40 sea urchins (see method)

4 tablespoons olive oil

1 small chilli, chopped

2 garlic cloves, chopped

2–3 very ripe cherry tomatoes, coarsely chopped

2 tablespoons coarsely chopped fresh parsley

400 g (14 oz) linguine

Salt and freshly ground black pepper

I was invited to judge a sea urchin fishing competition in Porto Badisco, one of the many small coastal towns in Puglia, right in Italy's boot heel. The sea urchins had a marvellous flavour and were mostly eaten raw or on pasta. If you fish the urchins yourself (be careful of the spikes), try to collect only the slightly purple and green ones, not the black ones as these are inedible.

METHOD

Handle the sea urchins with a cloth or wear gloves. To open them, insert kitchen scissors in the lower part of the urchin, cut away half the urchin and discard, keeping only the half with the coral-like roe attached. Clean between the lines of roe and use a teaspoon to scrape the roe into a bowl.

Heat the oil in a pan, add the chilli and garlic and fry briefly. Add the tomatoes and parsley and cook for a couple of minutes, then season. Remove from the heat.

Cook the pasta in a large pan of boiling salted water until *al dente*, then drain, reserving a couple of spoonfuls of the cooking water. Stir the reserved cooking water into the sauce, then add the pasta. Mix together and serve each portion topped with the sea urchin roe. Mix before eating to flavour the pasta.

SPAGHETTI IN PIAZZA
Spaghetti in the Square

SERVES 4

1 x 1 kg (2¼ lb) octopus

6 tablespoons virgin olive oil

1 x 300 g (11 oz) scorpion
   fish, cleaned

1 garlic clove, finely chopped

1 small chilli, finely chopped

800 g (1¾ lb) *polpa di
   pomodoro* (see page 15)

100 ml (3½ fl oz) dry white
   wine

500 g (4 lb 14 oz) spaghetti

2 tablespoons coarsely
   chopped fresh parsley

Salt

You need an appointment with certain fishermen in Sicily to go fishing at night with a lampara – *a huge light positioned on the bow of the boat in order to scrutinize the shallows. I was taken out in a small boat by two fishermen armed with harpoons. The sea should have been as smooth as oil but instead it was very rough, and all we managed to catch was an octopus and a scorpion fish. I had to improvise with them and this is the dish I cooked in the piazza for the fishermen. They enjoyed it, despite the meagre ingredients. Octopus is easily available; the scorpion fish can be replaced with pieces of monkfish if necessary.*

METHOD

Clean the octopus, removing the eyes and beak. Heat the olive oil in a large pan, add the octopus, scorpion fish, garlic, chilli and tomato pulp, then cover and cook on a gentle heat for 20 minutes. Remove the scorpion fish and octopus from the pan. Bone the scorpion fish and flake the flesh. Cut the octopus into chunks. Put the flesh of both back in the pan, add the wine and some salt and continue to cook slowly for 15–20 minutes, or until the octopus is tender. Add some water if the sauce gets too thick.

Cook the spaghetti in a large pan of boiling salted water until *al dente*, then drain and mix with the sauce. Sprinkle with the parsley and serve.

Following pages (from left):

Cavatelli con le Cozze (page 49);

*Orecchiette con Broccoli e
Prosciutto* (page 48)

CULURZONES
Sardinian Ravioli

SERVES 6–8

50 g (2 oz) butter

8 sage leaves

A pinch of saffron, dissolved
  in a little hot water

Freshly grated pecorino or
  Parmesan cheese, to serve

FOR THE FILLING

800 g (1¾ lb) potatoes,
  boiled and mashed

200 g (7 oz) fresh (*dolce*)
  pecorino cheese, grated

50 g (2 oz) aged pecorino
  cheese, grated

120 g (4½ oz) Parmesan
  cheese, freshly grated

2½ tablespoons extra virgin
  olive oil

2½ tablespoons finely
  chopped fresh mint

FOR THE DOUGH

300 g (11 oz) *doppio zero*
  (00) flour (see page 14)

1 egg yolk

About 120 ml (4 fl oz) water

It is interesting that two regions as far apart as Sardinia and the Veneto have a very similar way of shaping their home-made ravioli. Although the fillings are different, they both taste wonderful. You need a little patience to make culurzones *but the result is very rewarding.*

The great footballer Gianfranco Zola was delighted when I made this dish from his home town of Orlena in Sardinia as a surprise for him. Unfortunately, the setting was less traditional – the grounds of Chelsea Football Club.

METHOD

To make the filling, mix the potatoes with the cheeses, oil and mint, then set aside.

To make the dough, pile the flour up into a volcano shape on a work surface (marble is best) and make a large well in the centre. Put the egg yolk and water in the well, keeping back a little of the water in case you don't need it all. Lightly beat the egg yolk and water together with a fork and then gradually mix in the flour with your hands, adding more water if necessary, to make a soft dough. Knead the dough well with the palms of your hands for about 20 minutes, until smooth and elastic.

Roll out the pasta either by hand or with a pasta machine until it is very thin – about 2 mm (1/16 in). Cut out 10 cm (4 in) rounds. Knead the trimmings together, reroll and cut out more rounds.

To shape the *culurzones*, take a pasta round in one hand and place a teaspoonful of the filling mixture off centre on it. Turn up the bottom of the dough over the filling, then pinch a fold of dough over from the right and then the left side to give a pleated effect. Pinch the top together to seal. You should end up with a money-bag shape. Because the pasta is so thin it is important to work quickly and to keep the remaining pasta rounds covered to prevent drying.

Put the butter, sage leaves and saffron water in a large pan and heat gently until the butter has melted. Meanwhile, cook the *culurzones* in plenty of lightly salted boiling water until *al dente*. Drain and combine with the hot butter mixture, stirring to coat well. Serve either with more grated pecorino or with Parmesan, as you prefer.

Following pages:

Spaghetti in Piazza (page 51)

BUCATINI AGLIO E MUDDICA
Bucatini with Poor Man's Parmesan

SERVES 4

6 tablespoons virgin olive oil

1 garlic clove, finely chopped

6 anchovy fillets

1 tablespoon salted capers, soaked in water for 10 minutes, then drained and roughly chopped

400 g (14 oz) bucatini

½ quantity of *Aglio e Muddica* (see opposite)

Freshly ground black pepper

This Sicilian recipe is also eaten in Calabria. Sometimes plain bread-crumbs are toasted and used to add some 'grit' to pasta instead of aglio e muddica.

METHOD

Put the oil and garlic in a pan and cook extremely gently, without letting the garlic brown. Add the anchovies and capers and stir over a very gentle heat until the anchovies melt into the oil, then remove from the heat.

Cook the pasta in a large pan of boiling salted water until *al dente*, then drain, saving a couple of spoonfuls of the cooking water. Stir this into the anchovy sauce. Mix the pasta with the sauce, season with black pepper and sprinkle over the bread-crumb mixture.

AGLIO E MUDDICA
Poor Man's Parmesan

MAKES 200 g (7 oz)

200 g (7 oz) fresh
  breadcrumbs (best made
  from country-style bread
  that is 1–2 days' old)

½ garlic clove

1 tablespoon extra virgin
  olive oil

1 tablespoon very finely
  chopped fresh basil

Salt

Like many peasant dishes, this owes its invention to poverty. It was devised as a cheap substitute for Parmesan cheese, which used to be a rather expensive commodity reserved for the rich. In fact it is known as poor man's Parmesan. Nowadays, though, aglio e muddica *(garlic and breadcrumbs) offers a pleasant alternative to cheese and no longer deserves the name 'poor'. The breadcrumbs are cunningly flavoured with a little olive oil, garlic and basil and are kept dry and crumbly like grated cheese. It is essential to use Southern-style rustic bread made with durum wheat flour. The mixture can be sprinkled on pasta dishes, vegetables, meat and anything else you think it may complement. Ideal for people with an allergy to dairy products.*

METHOD

Rub the breadcrumbs through your fingers until they are the size of half a rice grain. Chop the garlic as finely as you can to obtain a paste, then mix it with the olive oil. Wet your fingers with a little of the oil and try to manipulate the breadcrumbs until all the oil has been incorporated and the crumbs become loose and not sticky. Add the basil and some salt and work with your fingers again to obtain a homogeneous mixture. Store in the fridge.

SPAGHETTI ALLA CARBONARA
Spaghetti Carbonara (with Eggs and Bacon)

SERVES 6

500 g (1 lb 2 oz) spaghetti or spaghettoni (the largest spaghetti)

25 g (1 oz) lard

25 g (1 oz) butter

2 tablespoons olive oil

1 garlic clove, slightly squashed

100 g (4 oz) pancetta or *guanciale* (see page 16), cut into small chunks

5 tablespoons dry white wine

5 eggs

100 g (4 oz) Parmesan cheese (or pecorino for the purists), freshly grated

3 tablespoons finely chopped fresh parsley

Salt and freshly ground black pepper

I include a recipe for this well-known dish because most people I know get it completely wrong, either adding milk or cream or letting the eggs become scrambled. This recipe is the real thing. It was brought to Lazio from Umbria by coal men (carbonari), *who came to sell charcoal to the Romans. Since then it has been adopted by the Romans and is famous worldwide.*

METHOD

Cook the pasta in a large pan of boiling salted water until *al dente*. Meanwhile, heat the lard, butter and oil in a pan and fry the garlic and pancetta or *guanciale* until crisp. Discard the garlic and add the white wine to the pan. Boil to evaporate it a little.

Lightly beat the eggs in a large bowl with the grated cheese, parsley and some salt and pepper. When the pasta is ready, drain and add to the egg mixture in the bowl, stirring to coat the pasta. Then add to the pancetta or *guanciale* in the pan. Stir a couple of times and then serve.

SPAGHETTI ALLA CARRETTIERA
Cart Drivers' Spaghetti

SERVES 4

25 g (1 oz) dried porcini
   mushrooms

4 tablespoons olive oil

1 garlic clove, crushed

50 g (2 oz) pancetta, finely
   chopped

200 g (7 oz) can of tuna in oil,
   drained

600 g (1 lb 5 oz) *pomodorini*
   (very sweet cherry
   tomatoes), chopped, or
   500 g (1 lb 2 oz) *polpa di
   pomodoro* (see page 15)

400 g (14 oz) Neapolitan
   spaghetti (see page 13)

Salt

Freshly ground black pepper
   (optional)

Freshly grated Parmesan
   cheese, to serve (optional)

Together with pizza, spaghetti is the symbol of Naples. To celebrate artisan spaghetti, here is a curious recipe that not only the Neapolitans but also the Sicilians and Romans claim as their own. The Neapolitan version is very simple and is named in honour of the cart drivers who used to deliver food and wine to big cities. I find the combination of porcini and tuna quite intriguing.

METHOD

Soak the porcini in warm water for 30 minutes, then drain and chop, reserving the soaking liquid.

Heat the olive oil in a frying pan, add the garlic and fry gently until softened. Add the pancetta and allow to brown a little. Stir in the porcini and tuna and fry for a few minutes, then add the tomatoes and some salt and simmer for 20 minutes. Stir in a few spoonfuls of the mushroom soaking liquid just to flavour the sauce and cook for about 5 minutes longer.

Meanwhile, cook the spaghetti in a large pan of boiling salted water until *al dente*, then drain and mix with the sauce. Season with black pepper and sprinkle with Parmesan cheese, if liked.

TIMBALLO DI RISO CON RIGAGLIE
Rice Timbale with Porcini and Giblet Ragù

SERVES 6

675 g (1½ lb) risotto rice

75 g (3 oz) Parmesan cheese, freshly grated

100 g (4 oz) butter

50 g (2 oz) dried breadcrumbs

FOR THE RAGÙ

120 ml (4 fl oz) virgin olive oil

300 g (11 oz) onions, finely sliced

675 g (1½ lb) mixed chicken giblets, including the gizzard, heart and liver, cut into small chunks

300 g (11 oz) fresh porcini mushrooms, chopped

25 g (1 oz) dried porcini mushrooms, soaked in hot water for 30 minutes, then drained and chopped

2 glasses of dry white wine

600 g (1 lb 5 oz) *polpa di pomodoro* (see page 15)

50 g (2 oz) tomato paste

3 tablespoons finely chopped fresh parsley

Salt and freshly ground black pepper

A genuine risotto can come only from Northern Italy, where they are masters at making it. All the other regions serve a type of risotto, however. This recipe from Rome is for a timbale rather than the usual creamy dish. The members of the Accademia Italiana della Cucina, who were my guests in Labica near Rome, greatly appreciated it. Use vialone nano rice if you can get it; it has a shorter, rounder grain than other varieties of risotto rice, which gives a nice consistency for this dish.

METHOD

Cook the rice in plenty of boiling salted water for about 6 minutes, then drain, leaving it a little moist. Mix with the Parmesan cheese and 75 g (3 oz) of the butter. Set aside.

Preheat the oven to 200°C, 400°F, Gas Mark 6.

To make the ragù, heat the oil in a pan, add the onions and fry briefly until softened. Then add the giblets and fry over a medium heat for 10 minutes, stirring all the time. Add the fresh porcini and the soaked dried ones and cook for a few minutes longer. Pour in the wine and let it bubble for a few minutes to evaporate, then stir in the tomato pulp and tomato paste. Season with salt and pepper and cook gently, uncovered, for about 20 minutes, until the mixture has a saucelike consistency – it should be loose but not too wet. Stir in the parsley.

Take a mould or ovenproof dish about 23 cm (9 in) in diameter and 15 cm (6 in) deep. Butter it and dust with the breadcrumbs, reserving some for the top of the timbale. Line the mould with most of the rice in a layer about 2 cm (¾ in) thick, making sure there is a good layer of rice on the sides so that it will hold the filling. Add the ragù and cover with the rest of the rice. Sprinkle with the remaining breadcrumbs and dot with the rest of the butter.

Bake the timbale in the oven for 15 minutes. Allow to cool slightly, then turn it out on to a serving plate. Should this operation become difficult, serve directly from the mould.

RISOTTO SARDO
Sardinian Risotto

SERVES 6

6 tablespoons olive oil

600 g (1 lb 5 oz) risotto rice

75 g (3 oz) aged pecorino cheese, grated

40 g (1½ oz) butter

Freshly ground black pepper

FOR THE RAGÙ

4 tablespoons olive oil

1 small onion, finely chopped

250 g (9 oz) minced lean pork or veal

1 small glass of red wine (preferably Sardinian Cannonau)

200 ml (7 fl oz) chicken stock

200 g (7 oz) *polpa di pomodoro* (see page 15)

¼ teaspoon good saffron powder

Salt

This risotto does not differ much in principle from the Spanish paella. Considering that Sardinia and Catalonia have many things in common, including some dialect, this is not so surprising. It is, however, very different from the Northern Italian risotto.

METHOD

First make the ragù. Heat the oil in a pan, add the onion and fry gently until softened. Then add the minced meat and fry until brown. Stir in the wine, stock, tomato pulp, saffron and some salt and simmer for 20–25 minutes. Remove from the heat and set the ragù aside.

For the risotto, heat the oil in a pan, add the rice and stir for about 5 minutes over a gentle heat to coat each grain with oil. Gradually add half the ragù and stir for 5 minutes. Keep an eye on the moisture level and add some hot water if necessary; the rice will absorb a lot of liquid. Add the rest of the ragù and stir for 10 minutes or until the rice is cooked. The consistency should be quite loose. Stir in the grated cheese, butter and some pepper. Leave to rest for a few minutes and then serve.

MALLOREDDUS
Sardinian Gnocchi with Tomato Sauce

SERVES 4

5 tablespoons extra virgin
olive oil

1 small onion, finely chopped

675 g (1½ lb) *polpa di
pomodoro* (see page 15) or
pomodorini (very sweet,
small tomatoes)

6 basil leaves

400 g (14 oz) malloreddus
pasta

50 g (2 oz) aged pecorino
cheese, grated

Salt and freshly ground black
pepper

*This pasta is still made by hand in Sardinia, using durum wheat flour,
saffron and water. It is also manufactured commercially now but
purists say the quality is inferior. If you want to make it yourself, take
350 g (12 oz) durum wheat flour, a pinch of salt and a sachet of good
Sardinian saffron diluted in a cup of warm water. Mix to a fairly stiff
dough and then knead for at least half an hour. Take a little of the
dough, roll it into a very thin baton and cut it into small pellets. Roll
the pasta pellets on a ridged piece of wood, rather like the tool for
making butter curls. The result is mini gnocchi, which have to be dried
out a little before use. It is easier to buy them ready made!*

METHOD

Heat the oil in a pan, add the onion and fry gently until softened.
Add the tomato pulp and cook gently for 20 minutes. Towards
the end of the cooking time, add the basil leaves and some salt
and pepper, plus a little water if the sauce is too thick.

Cook the pasta in a large pan of boiling salted water until *al
dente* (about 11–12 minutes), then drain. Mix in the sauce and
serve with the grated pecorino cheese.

PANELLE AL FORNO
Baked Chickpea Gnocchi

SERVES 4

1.5 litres (2½ pints) water

15 g (½ oz) salt

2 tablespoons coarsely chopped fresh parsley

250 g (9 oz) chickpea flour

50 g (2 oz) butter

1 teaspoon freshly grated nutmeg

40 g (1½ oz) Parmesan cheese, freshly grated

Freshly ground black pepper

Although this is similar in principle to gnocchi alla romana, *I find that chickpea flour makes much tastier gnocchi than semolina. In Palermo, where* panelle *are fried and eaten sandwiched in bread, they would undoubtedly approve.*

METHOD

Put the water in a pan with the salt and parsley and bring to the boil. Gradually pour in the chickpea flour, beating vigorously with a wire whisk to prevent lumps forming. Cook for 5 minutes, stirring, then pour the mixture on to an oiled surface and spread out in a layer 1 cm (½ in) thick. Leave to cool and set.

Preheat the oven to 200°C, 400°F, Gas Mark 6.

Cut the chickpea mixture into circles 4 cm (1½ in) in diameter and arrange them on an oiled baking tray, overlapping them slightly. Dot with the butter and sprinkle the nutmeg, Parmesan cheese and black pepper over the surface. Bake for 10 minutes, then place under a hot grill to brown the top.

I use up the bits of dough left after cutting out the circles by baking them with a fresh tomato and basil sauce. I hate throwing food away!

Following pages:

Panelle al Forno (above)

ZUPPA DI LENTICCHIE
Braised Lentils with Borage

SERVES 4

400 g (14 oz) lentils

2 garlic cloves, peeled but left whole

1.5 litres (2½ pints) chicken or vegetable stock

200 g (7 oz) cherry tomatoes, halved

225 g (8 oz) borage leaves, roughly chopped (save the blue flowers for decoration)

120 ml (4 fl oz) extra virgin olive oil

Salt and freshly ground black pepper

The translation of zuppa *as soup doesn't reflect the hearty nature of this lentil stew from Campania, which is one of several dishes from the area using the herb borage. Very simple, but very tasty indeed. Some people like to add a little chilli at the beginning but I prefer not to. Use Castelluccio lentils if you can get them, or Puy lentils.*

METHOD

Put the lentils, garlic and stock in a pan, bring to the boil and simmer for 15 minutes. Add the tomatoes and borage leaves and continue to cook until the lentils are tender. Season with salt and pepper. Serve in soup bowls with the olive oil drizzled over and decorated with the borage flowers.

PANZANELLA MARINARA
Summer Bread Salad

SERVES 4

8 slices of white, country-
style bread, dried in a low
oven

300 g (11 oz) cherry
tomatoes, cut into quarters

1 bunch of spring onions,
finely chopped

1 yellow pepper, cut into
small cubes

1 garlic clove, very finely
chopped

20 green olives, pitted and
halved

20 basil leaves, plus sprigs to
garnish

120 ml (4 fl oz) virgin olive oil

1 tablespoon strong red wine
vinegar

8 anchovy fillets, quartered

Salt and freshly ground black
pepper

Here is a simple recipe that includes all the elements of the healthy Mediterranean diet. The ingredients are almost always available in a Southern Italian household and do not cost very much. It is often made with frisella *(see page 14) but my mother used leftover bread, dried in the oven the better to absorb the juice of the ripe tomatoes. Ideal as a starter on a summer's day.*

METHOD

Soften the dried bread in a little cold water, then reduce it to coarse crumbs. Put the breadcrumbs, tomatoes, spring onions, yellow pepper, garlic, olives and basil leaves in a bowl and mix well. Add the olive oil and vinegar and season with salt and pepper. Mix very well to obtain a moist but not too wet mixture. Serve garnished with the anchovies and a sprig of basil.

Following pages (from left):

Panzanella Marinara (above);

Zuppa di Lenticchie (page 68)

PASTA E FAGIOLI DI ZIA DORA
Aunt Dora's Pasta and Bean Soup

SERVES 4

**300 g (11 oz) fresh cannellini
 beans (or 150 g (5 oz) dried
 beans, soaked in water
 overnight and then drained)**

**1.5 litres (2½ pints) stock
 (a cube will do)**

**2 very ripe small tomatoes,
 finely chopped**

4 tablespoons virgin olive oil

**2 garlic cloves, roughly
 chopped**

4 basil leaves

300 g (11 oz) tubettini pasta

**Salt and freshly ground black
 pepper**

**Extra virgin olive oil for
 drizzling**

This soup is served all over Italy but it varies from region to region – almost from family to family. The main differences between the Northern and Southern versions are that in the South cannellini beans are used instead of borlotti and the beans are not crushed to thicken the soup. Also, Southern Italians make it with olive oil rather than other fats, which means the soup can be eaten cold, as is customary during summer. This recipe takes me back to wartime, when I used to spend my holidays with my favourite aunt, Dora, in the province of Avellino.

METHOD

Place the beans in a large pan with the stock and tomatoes and bring to the boil. Cover and simmer until the beans are tender (about 1½–2 hours).

Heat the oil in a separate pan, add the garlic and fry until it is golden brown but not burnt. Stir this into the soup with the basil. Add the pasta and cook until the pasta is soft (not too *al dente* in this case). Serve with a drizzle of extra virgin olive oil, salt and plenty of black pepper.

If you use canned beans, start by frying the garlic in the oil, then add the tomatoes, stock and beans and bring to the boil. Add the pasta and basil and simmer until the pasta is cooked.

MARIOLA
Omelette Soup

SERVES 4

6 eggs

2 tablespoons dried
breadcrumbs

4 tablespoons pecorino or
Parmesan cheese, freshly
grated

2 tablespoons very finely
chopped fresh parsley

4 tablespoons olive oil

1 litre (1¾ pints) good
chicken or beef stock

Salt and freshly ground black
pepper

I was astonished to come across this soup in Calabria, since it is very similar to one I used to love while studying in Vienna. The Viennese speciality is called Fritatensuppe. *Both have as their base a good chicken or beef broth and are garnished with a thin omelette cut into strips. Remarkably tasty and very easy to make.*

METHOD

Beat the eggs in a bowl and then mix in the breadcrumbs, cheese, parsley, salt and plenty of pepper. Heat the olive oil in a frying pan and make 5 or 6 (depending on the size of the pan) very thin, flat omelettes. Turn out of the pan and cut into very narrow, small strips.

Heat the stock in a pan until it is piping hot, add the omelette strips and serve. You could sprinkle a little grated cheese on top.

baking and frying

The sight of old country houses in the South with purpose-built wood-fired ovens just outside suggests good living. These ovens used to be lit once a week to bake the family's supply of bread – and occasionally pizza, savoury or sweet tarts and cakes as well. The flavour imparted to food exposed to the smoke and smell of burnt wood is one of the most warming and desirable things in the culinary world.

From *bruschetta* to *panzanella*, bread is a basic commodity that Italians cannot do without. Every region has its own specialities, resulting in a wonderfully inviting choice. Pizza is the baked food *par excellence*. The best ones are baked in a wood-fired oven and every good pizzeria in Naples, the home of pizza, is equipped with one of these. Naples even has a pizza-making academy. In domestic ovens Southern Italians bake all sorts of dishes, from pasta timbales to stuffed vegetables. For simple vegetable dishes, or for rabbit, lamb and especially chicken, which are usually baked with potatoes, baking is a great liberation from constant checking during the cooking period. The exact cooking time is not important and the results are always extremely tasty. Furthermore, most dishes like these can be reheated without loss of flavour.

The other highly popular cooking method in the South is frying, for which Italians use at least two different types of oil – a simple olive oil and a cheaper one such as sunflower. The distinctive taste imparted by frying in olive oil is essential to many Southern dishes. Sometimes, however, depending on the dish, lard is used to contribute its own special flavour.

The tradition of frying probably comes from Arab countries, where it is a very common quick cooking method. The advantage of frying is that once the initial

Previous pages: *Pasta Cresciuta* (page 94)

preparation is done, the food can be ready to eat in minutes. Calzone, a folded pizza where the dough envelops the filling, can be fried or baked. It makes ideal fast food and is available throughout the South. *Arancini* (see page 91), small stuffed balls of rice coated in breadcrumbs and deep-fried, are also fast food and are mostly eaten standing up in bars for lunch.

Naturally, most fried foods are better eaten crisp and hot, particularly meat, offal and vegetables, but some, especially sweet ones, can be eaten cold – *Struffoli*, for example (see page 180), which are little knobs of pastry, deep-fried and then flavoured with honey and candied peel. To prevent fried food being greasy, always make sure the oil is hot enough and drain the food on absorbent paper immediately you lift it from the pan.

There are so many fried specialities in the South. Perhaps the epitome of frying is the *fritto misto*, which may consist of various pieces of meat and vegetables, or may be a *fritto misto di pesce*, the seafood version, of which there exist as many varieties as there are places by the sea. Usually, however, it contains small octopus, squid, prawns, small fish and perhaps eel. Eaten under a pergola by the sea, accompanied by a good glass of chilled white wine, this constitutes one of those moments you will always remember after your return from holiday.

PEPERONI, MELANZANE E ZUCCHINI RIPIENI
Stuffed Peppers, Aubergines and Courgettes

SERVES 4

1 yellow pepper

1 red pepper

2 small aubergines

2 courgettes

200 g (7 oz) stale bread, crusts removed

1 egg, beaten

3 tablespoons finely chopped fresh parsley

150 g (5 oz) Parma ham, cut into small cubes

1 garlic clove, finely chopped

150 g (5 oz) caciocavallo cheese, cut into small cubes

150 g (5 oz) pecorino cheese, cut into small cubes

2 tablespoons freshly grated Parmesan cheese

Olive oil for drizzling

Salt and freshly ground black pepper

This popular vegetable dish is served as a main course in Southern Italy, as well as an antipasto *or snack. Any vegetable that makes a suitable container can be stuffed with a variety of fillings. My mother always used to bake more stuffed vegetables than she needed and they made an excellent midnight feast when my brothers and I returned home and raided the fridge.*

This version is not for vegetarians, unless you omit the ham.

METHOD

Preheat the oven to 200°C, 400°F, Gas Mark 6.

Cut the peppers in half down through the centre, including the stalk. Clean out the seeds and cut out the membranes with a sharp knife. Cut the aubergines and the courgettes in half lengthways and carefully scoop out the flesh (a melon baller is good for this), leaving a boat-shaped vegetable.

Soften the bread briefly in a little water and then squeeze it dry and make it into fine crumbs. Mix thoroughly with the egg, parsley, ham, garlic, cheeses and some salt and pepper. Fill the cavities of the vegetables with this mixture, packing it in loosely rather than pressing it down. Place the stuffed vegetables on an oiled baking tray, drizzle each one generously with olive oil and bake for 35 minutes, until the vegetables are tender and the filling is browned. Serve hot, warm or cold.

PASTA AL FORNO
Baked Pasta

SERVES 8

800 g (1¾ lb) pasta, such as maccheroni, ziti or penne

450 g (1 lb) mozzarella cheese, cut into small cubes

200 g (7 oz) Parmesan cheese, freshly grated

FOR THE SAUCE

100 ml (3½ fl oz) olive oil

1 onion, finely chopped

1 garlic clove, finely chopped

500 g (1 lb 2 oz) chicken livers and hearts

400 g (14 oz) fresh porcini, chopped or 400 g (14 oz) of cultivated mushrooms plus 25 g (1 oz) dried porcini, soaked in warm water for 30 minutes, then drained

1 small glass of white wine

1 kg (2¼ lb) ripe tomatoes, deseeded and chopped, or 800 g (1¾ lb) *polpa di pomodoro* (see page 15)

2 tablespoons chopped fresh basil

Salt and freshly ground black pepper

This is a dish for grand occasions, such as weddings or Christmas. The pasta itself is only a vehicle for all sorts of goodies, resulting in a rich timbale. The curious thing is that at festive events it is customary to enjoy richer food than usual anyway, and so only a small wedge of this dish is eaten. The rest makes a welcome leftover the following evening. Some gourmet Neapolitans add fresh truffles but I think that is going a little too far...

METHOD

To make the sauce, heat the oil in a large pan and fry the onion and garlic until softened. Add the chicken livers and hearts and cook over a medium heat for 15 minutes, stirring all the time. Add the mushrooms and cook for a few minutes. Pour in the wine and boil to evaporate a little. Add the tomatoes and basil and cook gently for 40 minutes. Season to taste.

Preheat the oven to 200°C, 400°F, Gas Mark 6.

Cook the pasta in a large pan of boiling salted water for half its normal cooking time, then drain and mix with a little of the sauce. Take a round or square 25–30 cm (10–12 in) baking tin or ovenproof dish about 7.5 cm (3 in) deep and, commencing with pasta, build layers of pasta and sauce, scattering mozzarella cubes and grated Parmesan in between. Finish with sauce and Parmesan cheese. Bake for 25 minutes and then serve.

PIZZA MARINARA
Pizza with Anchovies

MAKES 4

FOR THE DOUGH

25 g (1 oz) fresh yeast or
  15 g (½ oz) dried yeast
300 ml (10 fl oz) lukewarm
  water
A pinch of salt
2 tablespoons olive oil
600 g (1 lb 5 oz) *doppio zero*
  (00) flour (see page 14)

FOR THE TOMATO SAUCE

2 tablespoons olive oil
1 garlic clove, finely chopped
400 g (14 oz) can of chopped
  tomatoes
4 basil leaves
Salt and freshly ground black
  pepper

FOR THE TOPPING

36 anchovy fillets
1 tablespoon salted capers,
  soaked in water for
  10 minutes, then drained
4 garlic cloves, finely
  chopped
1 tablespoon dried oregano
A handful of black olives
120 ml (4 fl oz) olive oil

Of the endless variety of pizzas, my favourites are the simple Margherita and the Marinara, which is the tastiest because of the anchovies.

METHOD

First make the dough. Dissolve the yeast in the water, then stir in the salt and olive oil. Heap up the flour in a mound on a work surface and make a well in the centre. Pour in the yeast mixture and mix with your hands until all the liquid has been absorbed by the flour. Knead the dough for 10–15 minutes, until smooth and elastic. Sprinkle a little flour in a large bowl, put the dough in it and spread a little oil over the top to prevent a crust forming. Cover the bowl with a dry cloth and leave to rise in a warm, draught-free place for 1 hour or until the dough has doubled in size.

Meanwhile, make the tomato sauce. Heat the olive oil in a pan, add the garlic and fry gently for a minute or two. Stir in the chopped tomatoes and simmer for 15 minutes, until thickened. Season with salt and pepper and stir in the basil leaves, torn into pieces.

Preheat the oven to 230°C, 450°F, Gas Mark 8.

Knock back the risen dough and divide it into 4. Roll each piece into a ball and then press it out with your hands, starting from the middle, until it is about 5 mm (¼ in) thick. It's a good idea to make the edges slightly thicker to prevent the topping running away.

Place each pizza base on a baking sheet or in an oiled 25–28 cm (10–11 in) round pizza pan. Spread with the tomato sauce, then arrange the anchovies on top. Scatter over the capers, chopped garlic and oregano and put a few olives in the centre of each pizza. Drizzle the olive oil over the whole surface and season with freshly ground black pepper – do not add salt as the anchovies and capers are salty enough. Bake the pizzas in the preheated oven for 10 minutes. Delicious hot or even cold.

PANE CASERECCIO
Rustic Pugliese Bread

MAKES 1 LARGE LOAF

25 g (1 oz) fresh yeast or
15 g (½ oz) dried yeast
175 ml (6 fl oz) lukewarm
water
2 teaspoons salt
1 teaspoon coarsely ground
black pepper
3 tablespoons virgin olive oil
2 eggs, beaten
600 g (1 lb 5 oz) *doppio zero*
(00) flour (see page 14)
150 g (5 oz) leftover salami,
cut into small cubes
150 g (5 oz) leftover cheese,
cut into small cubes
2 tablespoons dried
breadcrumbs

Nothing is thrown away in an Italian kitchen. Housewives often create works of art with leftovers! Pane casereccio *is made using all sorts of leftovers of cheese and meat which are still good to eat but too tough to slice. You can use any type of hard cheese, from grated Parmesan to pecorino, provolone or scamorza. Oddments of salami, ham or sausages can also be included.*

METHOD

Dissolve the yeast in the water in a small bowl, then stir in the salt, pepper, oil and beaten eggs. Put the flour into a large bowl, make a well in the centre and pour in the yeast mixture. Mix well to make a dough. Knead for at least 20 minutes, until smooth and elastic. Sprinkle over the salami and cheese and gently knead them into the dough. With your hands, shape the dough into a longish sausage, then join both ends together to make a ring. Carefully transfer this to a baking tray dusted with the bread-crumbs. Cover and leave in a warm, draught-free place for 20 minutes, until slightly risen.

Preheat the oven to 200°C, 400°F, Gas Mark 6.

Bake the loaf for 35 minutes, until it is golden brown on top and sounds hollow when tapped underneath.

MOZZARELLA FRITTA
Fried Mozzarella

SERVES 4

2 mozzarella, preferably
   buffalo, cut into slices
   1 cm (½ in) thick
Plain flour for dusting
2 eggs, beaten with some salt
   and freshly ground black
   pepper
Dried breadcrumbs for
   coating
Olive oil for shallow-frying

This simple snack is easy to prepare yet it is a very flavoursome morsel that lifts the spirits. It is similar to the better-known mozzarella in carrozza, *but lighter because there is no bread.*

METHOD

Lightly coat the mozzarella slices in flour and then dip them in the beaten egg. Coat with breadcrumbs. Heat some olive oil in a large pan over a moderate heat and fry the mozzarella until it starts to melt, turning the slices once. It is a very quick process. Serve immediately.

PANE CARASAU
O CARTA DI MUSICA
Sardinian Crispy Bread

MAKES 16 SHEETS

20 g (¾ oz) fresh yeast
About 500 ml (18 fl oz)
   lukewarm water
A pinch of salt
1 kg (2¼ lb) durum wheat
   flour (not too finely milled,
   but finer then semolina)

This thin, crunchy bread, which looks like music manuscript paper (hence its name), is perhaps the most striking recipe I have found during my latest journey around Southern Italy. Of unknown ancient origins, it used to be made in vast quantities for sailors to take on long voyages or for shepherds who lived in the mountains during summer. Its versatility is remarkable. Wrapped in cloth it keeps for months and can be eaten plain; drizzled with olive oil and baked briefly to make it even crispier; broken up and served with milk like cornflakes; used to make lasagne; moistened in stock and topped with tomatoes, grated pecorino and a poached egg (when it is known as pane frattau); or simply soft-ened with water and rolled up with whatever filling you fancy.

Because making this bread requires some skill – and, ideally a wood-fired oven – I recommend buying the hand-made version available in good Italian delicatessens. However, here is the recipe in case you would like to give it a go.

METHOD

Dissolve the yeast in the water and then stir in the salt. Heap up the flour in a mound on a work surface and make a well in the centre. Pour in the yeast mixture and gradually draw in the flour until you have a fairly firm dough. Knead for 10–15 minutes, until smooth, then shape into 8 balls and place them on a floured board. Cover with a cloth and leave until doubled in size.

With a rolling pin, roll out each ball of dough, starting from the centre, into a circle about 3 mm (⅛ in) thick. Leave to rest for 1½ hours.

Preheat the oven to 220°C, 425°F, Gas Mark 7.

Transfer the dough circles to baking sheets and bake one by one for about a minute until they puff up to the size of a cushion. To help the dough puff up you should keep moving it around on the baking sheet with a palette knife and turn it over half way through cooking. Remove from the oven, deflate by pressing with your hand and then cut horizontally in half to make 2 even thinner sheets. Toast these in the oven until crisp, stack them up, then leave to cool. Wrap and store in a cool, dry place.

Following pages (from left):

Pizza Marinara (page 80);

Pane Casereccio (page 81)

CROCCHETTE ALLE MANDORLE
Potato Croquettes with Almonds

SERVES 4–6

500 g (1 lb 2 oz) potatoes

1 egg

**100 g (4 oz) Parmesan
  cheese, freshly grated**

**100 g (4 oz) blanched
  almonds, toasted and
  coarsely chopped**

150 ml (5 fl oz) olive oil

**Salt and freshly ground black
  pepper**

*An extremely tasty and useful alternative to plain potato croquettes.
Serve as an accompaniment to fish or meat.*

METHOD

Wash the potatoes well but don't peel them. Put them in a pan of water, bring to the boil and simmer until tender. Drain and leave to cool, then peel and mash them. Mix in the egg, Parmesan cheese and some salt and pepper, then shape into croquettes about 7.5 cm (3 in) long and 2.5 cm (1 in) thick.

Spread the chopped almonds out on a plate and roll the potato croquettes in them. Heat the oil in a frying pan and fry the croquettes over a medium heat until golden brown. Serve hot or cold.

FRITTO DI POLIPETTI
Deep-fried Baby Octopus

SERVES 6

1 kg (2¼ lb) small octopuses

Plain flour for dusting

Olive oil for deep-frying

Salt and freshly ground black pepper

Lemon wedges, to serve (optional)

Fried fish is popular in all the coastal areas of Italy. The simplest cooking method is to dust very fresh and tender seafood in flour and then fry it until crisp – ideal for a summer lunch with a fresh tomato salad, good bread and chilled white wine. The small octopuses I used for this recipe were so clean they did not need to be cleaned inside at all.

METHOD

Wash the octopuses and drain well. Dust them with flour, shaking off any excess, and deep-fry immediately in hot olive oil for no more than 3 minutes, until golden. Season to taste and serve with lemon wedges, if liked.

Following pages (from left):

Fritto di Polipetti (above);

Anguilla alla Romana (page 142)

FRITTATA DI PEPERONI VERDI
Green Pepper Omelette

SERVES 4

12 free range eggs

2 tablespoons very finely chopped fresh parsley

50 g (2 oz) Parmesan cheese, freshly grated

6 tablespoons olive oil

4 large green peppers, deseeded and cut into 8 slices, or if possible 500 g (1 lb 2 oz) small peppers

Salt and freshly ground black pepper

In the South it is very common to make an omelette for supper with courgettes, onions, asparagus and many other vegetables. Ideally this recipe should be made with the very small green peppers that look like chillies, but taste very sweet. Easier to find are the normal green peppers, which taste like grass when cooked. This dish can be served as a main course or in smaller slices, as an antipasto.

METHOD

Beat the eggs in a bowl and add the parsley, Parmesan cheese, salt and pepper. Heat the oil in a large frying pan and gently fry the slices of pepper until they begin to soften. If using small peppers, fry them whole without deseeding them. Pour in the egg mixture and cook over a medium heat until set and lightly browned underneath. Turn to cook the other side. Serve warm or at room temperature, cut into wedges.

ARANCINI
Rice Balls

MAKES 8

300 g (11 oz) arborio rice

**200 g (7 oz) mixture of
mozzarella and fresh
(*dolce*) pecorino cheese,
cut into cubes**

**50 g (2 oz) Parmesan cheese,
freshly grated**

**50 g (2 oz) butter, cut into
8 cubes**

2 eggs, beaten

**Dried breadcrumbs for
coating**

**Plenty of lard or olive oil for
deep-frying**

**Salt and freshly ground black
pepper**

One of the most popular rice specialities is the arancino di riso, *which comes from Sicily and is now available everywhere. Sold as fast food in cafés and delicatessens, it is called* arancino *because it is the size and shape of an orange. There are two types, filled with either ragù or cheese. Ideally they are best eaten fresh but, with the advent of microwaves in Italy, they are now usually served warmed up. Here is the cheese version.*

METHOD

Preheat the oven to 220°C, 425°F, Gas Mark 7.

Cook the rice in boiling salted water for 12 minutes or until 'al dente' and then drain. Mix the mozzarella and pecorino with the grated Parmesan and some black pepper.

Divide the rice into 8 equal parts. Wet your hands, then take a portion of the rice and line the palm of your hand with it, 2 cm (¾ in) thick, to make a mould that you can put the filling in. Place some of the cheese mixture and one cube of butter in the middle. Close your hand to make a ball, ensuring that the filling is completely enclosed by the rice. Press the rice together to shape the ball. Season the beaten eggs, then gently roll the rice balls in them. Next coat them completely in breadcrumbs and then deep-fry in lard or olive oil over a medium heat until the *arancini* are golden. Place them in the oven for 8 minutes to brown them further and ensure the filling is melted, then serve immediately.

Following pages:

*Peperoni, Melanzane e Zucchini
Ripieni* (page 78)

PASTA CRESCIUTA
Mixed Fritters

SERVES 6–8

24 sun-dried tomato halves

12–16 courgette flowers

24 large sage leaves

24 anchovy fillets

Olive oil for deep-frying

FOR THE BATTER

20 g (¾ oz) fresh yeast

315 ml (10½ fl oz) lukewarm
  water

300 g (11 oz) *doppio zero*
  (00) flour (see page 14)

A pinch of salt

Italians eat a great deal of fried food, cooking it almost exclusively in good olive oil, which gives an excellent flavour. These fritters make ideal party food since, although they are best eaten warm, they also taste good cold. In Naples they are called pasta cresciuta *– literally translated as 'grown dough' – because the yeast makes them rise. Many other ingredients can be fried in the same way – it's a challenge to come up with different ones.*

METHOD

To make the batter, dissolve the yeast in the water, then sift the flour and salt into a bowl, make a well in the centre and add the yeast mixture. Beat well with a whisk until you have a thick batter. Cover and leave in a warm place to rise for 1 hour or until almost doubled in size.

Soften the sun-dried tomatoes by soaking them in warm water for half an hour, then drain and pat dry. Shake out any dust or insects from the courgette flowers.

Heat plenty of olive oil in a large, deep pan over a medium-high heat. Dip each item into the batter, then put immediately in the hot oil and fry until puffed up and golden brown. The sage leaves are better dipped in separately and then sandwiched together in pairs. The anchovy fillets have to be put on the surface of the batter and scooped out with a spoon before frying. When the fritters are done, drain on absorbent paper and serve immediately.

CALZONCINI O PANZEROTTI
Small Fried Calzoni

MAKES 12

**1 quantity of pizza dough
(see page 80)**

**400 g (14 oz) mozzarella
cheese, cut into small cubes**

200 g (7 oz) ricotta cheese

**100 g (4 oz) Parmesan
cheese, freshly grated**

**1 tablespoon finely chopped
fresh basil**

Olive oil for deep-frying

**Salt and freshly ground black
pepper**

The baked calzone or, as I call it, the inverted pizza, has become popular worldwide wherever there are pizzerias. However, I am very fond of the Neapolitan fried calzoni because they are quicker to make and more fun. They are also known as panzerotti, *from* panza, *meaning tummy, because they puff up while frying. This is a lean version, made with just cheese, but the original also contains prosciutto and salame.*

METHOD

Knock back the risen dough and divide it into 12 balls. Roll each one out into a thin circle, 15 cm (6 in) in diameter.

Mix together the cheeses, basil and some salt and pepper. Put this filling on one half of each circle and then fold over the other half, pinching the edges together to seal. Deep-fry in plenty of hot olive oil until crisp and brown on each side, by which time the cheese should have melted.

Knowing that Southern Italians enjoy a healthy Mediterranean diet, one wonders where they put all the meat they consume after the *antipasto* and *primo*. However, meat is never served in large portions because the *secondo* is only one stage in the meal rather than the main event. Beef and veal are only occasionally eaten in the South, which lacks the rich pastures of the North. Sometimes buffalo meat is eaten and it is apparently very tasty indeed, but most buffalo are kept purely for their milk to make mozzarella.

The meats most frequently eaten in the South are lamb and mutton, with a little competition from goat. Pork, either fresh or preserved (see page 15), is also very common. Poultry is almost always chicken, although limited amounts of duck, geese and turkey are consumed, too. Horsemeat is available from specialist butchers, especially in Puglia, and is eaten mainly in the summer as it reputedly keeps well in hot weather. Knowing the reluctance of most of my readers to consume this type of meat I have not included any recipes for it in this book! However, it is usually eaten either grilled or stewed. And here we come to the general culinary preference of the Southerner, which is for tender meat to be charcoal-grilled and the tougher cuts to be stewed – usually with tomatoes to make a rich sauce that is served with pasta while the meat follows separately as a main course. Naples is famous for its ragù, made by slow-cooking beef, pork or lamb in a tomato sauce, releasing all the wonderful juices for an excellent flavour. Roasts are usually cooked with potatoes or artichokes, which are then served as tasty side dishes. Wine is not often used in cooking meat; *Scaloppine al Marsala Secco* (see page 105) is an exception, although this dish originated not in Sicily, as you might expect, but in the North, where veal is more readily available.

Previous pages: *Arrosto di Maiale con Patate all'Aglio* (page 104)

Offal is popular everywhere. Tripe is cooked in lots of different ways, especially in Rome and Naples. The other regions prefer heart, lung, liver, spleen and even testicles, which are wrapped up in a piece of intestine and then grilled. Specialities such as boiled tripe and grilled intestines are cooked with lots of spices and sold by the roadside. They are extremely tasty and offer a culinary reminder of the area's impoverished past, when the offal of pork or lamb was very cheap.

Last but not least, several types of game are very much enjoyed, although unfortunately they are becoming less and less readily available due to overhunting. Pigeon, hare and various passing birds are hunted seasonally and eaten with relish. However, game seldom appears in the shops; instead it goes straight to the hunter's family and friends. Quail are easier to buy, since they are farmed. Wild boar is still one of the main attractions in the cuisine of Sardinia where, despite being surrounded by the most beautiful sea, the population traditionally consumes lots of meat rather than fish.

BRACIOLE D'ABBACCHIO CON CARCIOFI
Lamb Cutlets with Artichokes

SERVES 4

16 small artichokes

8 lamb chops

6 tablespoons olive oil

1 garlic clove, finely chopped

1 small onion, finely chopped

1 sprig of marjoram

2 glasses of dry white wine

250 ml (8 fl oz) chicken stock

Salt and freshly ground black pepper

The combination of lamb and artichokes is always associated with Lazio, and particularly with Rome. Here is a very simple but effective recipe. If you are unable to find the very tender, small artichokes used in Rome, then use larger ones, removing the chokes and cutting the hearts into quarters.

METHOD

Cut the top third off each artichoke and discard the tough outer leaves until you reach the tender heart. Peel the stems. Keep in acidulated water to prevent discoloration.

Season the chops and fry them in the olive oil (originally lard was used) until browned on both sides. Remove from the pan and set aside. Add the garlic and onion to the pan and fry gently for a few minutes, until softened. Stir in the marjoram sprig, artichokes, wine and stock. Bring to a simmer, then cover the pan and cook for 10 minutes, until the artichokes are tender. Return the chops to the pan and cook gently for 10 minutes on a lower heat. Adjust the seasoning and serve immediately.

AGNELLO CON FINOCCHIO AL MARSALA
Lamb with Fennel and Marsala

SERVES 4

12 best end of neck lamb
cutlets

Plain flour for dusting

Olive oil for frying

1 garlic clove, finely chopped

1 fennel bulb and its leaves,
cut into small chunks

1 glass of vintage dry
Marsala

Salt and freshly ground black
pepper

After visiting the amazing Florio company, one of the oldest producers of Marsala in Sicily, and tasting some of its rare vintages, I appreciated how suitable this strong wine was not only for making scaloppine *and* zabaglione *but also for partnering with lamb. This dish could be made with rabbit or chicken, too. Leafy wild fennel grows in abundance in Sicily but it can be replaced here with bulb fennel. The combination of flavours is unusual but very good.*

METHOD

Dust the lamb cutlets in flour, shaking off any excess. Heat a little olive oil in a large frying pan and fry the cutlets on both sides until brown. Remove from the pan and set aside. Add the garlic and fennel to the pan and fry for a few minutes, stirring. Add the Marsala and some salt and pepper, then return the cutlets to the pan. Cook gently for 15 minutes and then serve.

Toasting the success of the Florio company, one of the oldest producers of Marsala in Sicily

AGNELLO BRODETTATO
Lamb with Egg Sauce

SERVES 4

6 tablespoons extra virgin
 olive oil

1 large onion, sliced

900 g (2 lb) boned leg of
 lamb, cut into fairly large
 chunks

1 glass of dry white wine

1 egg

3 egg yolks

2 tablespoons coarsely
 chopped fresh parsley

Juice of ½ lemon

Salt and freshly ground black
 pepper

Matera is one of the most interesting cities in Basilicata. Its ancient origins are still visible in the ruins of the Sassi, a conglomerate of houses built from tufa stone. Even more interesting are the chiese rupestri, *rural churches carved out of the same stone. These churches, some with original frescoes dating back a thousand years, were used as shelters, dwelling places and even wine cellars. The food I prepared for the architect who supervises the restoration of the city reflects the cuisine of the area. Try this recipe; it is simple and most appetizing.*

METHOD

Heat the oil in a large pan, add the onion and cook gently until tender. Add the meat and fry for 5 minutes, until browned. Stir in the wine and some salt and pepper, then cover and braise for 20–30 minutes, until the lamb is tender, stirring occasionally to prevent sticking.

Lightly beat the whole egg and egg yolks in a bowl, then add the parsley and lemon juice. Take the pan off the heat and pour in the egg mixture, stirring to obtain a silky-smooth sauce; the heat of the meat will gently cook the eggs but they should not scramble. Serve immediately, with bread.

SALSICCIA FRESCA
Freshly Made Sausages

SERVES 4–6

3 metres (3¼ yards) natural
   sausage casing

1.25 kg (2½ lb) lean pork

300 g (11 oz) pork back fat

25 g (1 oz) salt

1 teaspoon freshly ground
   black pepper

1 teaspoon fennel seeds

300 g (11 oz) caciocavallo or
   provola cheese, cut into
   small cubes

Dried chilli, to taste (optional)

Here you can try making your own sausages, as long as you can get sausage casing from your butcher and a little gadget with which to inject the filling; otherwise use a piping bag. You can, of course, include different seasonings such as garlic, onion or herbs to suit your own taste. However, I find this recipe (from Puglia) very appealing.

METHOD

Rinse the sausage casing in cold water and then leave it to soak in plenty of water for 2 hours. Drain well.

Coarsely mince the pork and fat and mix it with all the remaining ingredients. Attach one end of the casing to a sausage maker and push the meat mixture through, making sure the casing is well filled and there are no air gaps. Twist to make links. The sausages can be chargrilled, fried or even boiled. Serve with *Pepolata* (see page 163).

ARROSTO DI MAIALE CON PATATE ALL'AGLIO
Roast Pork with Potatoes and Garlic

SERVES 8

3 kg (7 lb) loin of pork

150 ml (5 fl oz) olive oil

1.5 kg (3¼ lb) small new potatoes

10 garlic cloves, unpeeled

4 sprigs of rosemary

Salt and freshly ground black pepper

Roast pork always makes a welcome meal for any lover of good food. The taste is distinctive and, when it is accompanied by complementary flavours such as garlic and rosemary, you can't go wrong. My favourite cut is the loin, which has enough skin to make plenty of delicious crackling.

METHOD

Preheat the oven to 200°C, 400°F, Gas Mark 6.

Score the pork skin with a small sharp knife in order to make crackling. Rub the whole joint with some of the olive oil and with salt and pepper. Place in a large roasting tin, cover with aluminium foil and roast for 30 minutes. Add the potatoes, garlic and rosemary sprigs to the tin. Drizzle them with the remaining olive oil, season with salt and pepper and bake without the foil for another 1½ hours, basting occasionally. Test the meat by piercing with a skewer; if the juices run clear it is done. Leave to rest for 15 minutes and then serve.

Antonio and friends enjoy a meal of *porceddu* (roast piglet) in the mountains of La Barbagia, Sardinia

SCALOPPINE AL MARSALA SECCO
Veal Escalopes with Marsala

SERVES 4

500 g (1 lb 2 oz) veal escalopes, cut 5 mm (¼ in) thick

Plain flour for dusting

6 tablespoons extra virgin olive oil or 50 g (2 oz) butter

1 glass of vintage dry Marsala

Salt and freshly ground black pepper

I cooked this in Calatafimi, the Sicilian town where Garibaldi's victory helped initiate the unification of Italy in 1860. An appropriate dish for such a historic spot, it combines veal, popular in the North, with Marsala, the pride of Sicily. Escalopes of chicken or turkey, or even fish such as monkfish or John Dory, can be substituted for the veal.

METHOD

Dust the escalopes in flour on both sides, shaking off any excess. Heat the oil or butter in a large, heavy frying pan. Fry the veal for a couple of minutes on each side, cooking it in batches so as not to overcrowd the pan. When all the escalopes are done, put them all back in the pan and add the wine and some seasoning. Stir for a few seconds; the meat should become lightly glazed because of the combination of flour and wine. Serve immediately, with *Peperoni alla Siciliana* (see page 162).

UCCELLINI DI CAMPO ALLO SPIEDO
False Birds on a Skewer

SERVES 4

600 g (1 lb 5 oz) veal fillet, cut into 16 thin slices

8 thin slices of Parma ham, cut in half

16 sage leaves

12 small cubes of white country-style bread, about 4 cm (1½ in) square

4 tablespoons olive oil

Juice of 1 lemon

Salt and freshly ground black pepper

It used to be common to eat sparrows in Italy, until the protests of bird lovers and an increasing concern for wildlife made eating small birds virtually obsolete. However, the custom still persists in a few areas, especially in Lombardia and the Veneto, where they are roasted and eaten with polenta. Here, thin slices of veal are rolled up to make small faggots in a shape similar to sparrows but, in my opinion, tastier.

METHOD

Trim the veal slices to rectangles about 4 x 7.5 cm (1½ x 3 in). Lay them out on a work surface and season with salt and pepper. Put a half slice of Parma ham on each one, then a sage leaf, and roll up tightly. Thread the rolls on 4 skewers, alternating them with the cubes of bread.

Mix the olive oil and lemon juice together. Grill the skewers slowly, basting them from time to time with the oil and lemon, for about 15–20 minutes, until the corners of the bread are browned and the veal is cooked.

SPALLA DI CAPRETTO FARCITA
Stuffed Shoulder of Kid with Truffle

SERVES 4

800 g (1¾ lb) very tender shoulder of kid, boned but with the small bone left in

½ teaspoon dried thyme, reduced to a powder

½ teaspoon dried rosemary, reduced to a powder

1 garlic clove, crushed

100 g (4 oz) pecorino cheese, thinly sliced

50 g (2 oz) black truffle, very thinly sliced

3 tablespoons extra virgin olive oil

1 glass of dry white wine

Salt and freshly ground black pepper

This was Antonino Colonna's contribution when we cooked in his excellent restaurant to please the palates of the board of the Accademia Italiana della Cucina of Rome. It can also be made using chicken breasts, pheasant or young lamb. Try to get the winter black truffle (Tuber melanosporum), which has more flavour than the summer one.

METHOD

Open out the meat and bat it out a little to flatten it. Sprinkle with the thyme, rosemary, garlic and some salt and pepper. Spread the slices of pecorino and truffle over the meat. Roll it up tightly in a piece of aluminium foil and secure both ends by twisting the foil. Put the roll in a pan with the olive oil, wine and a glass of water. Cover with a lid and simmer for 30 minutes. Remove the meat from the pan and leave to cool, then chill for at least 1 hour. Reserve the liquid.

To serve, remove the foil and return the meat to the cooking liquid. Heat through gently but thoroughly and serve sliced, with some of the liquid. It can also be served cold.

Following pages: *Uccellini di Campo allo Spiedo* (page 106); *Salsiccia Fresca* (page 103) on a bed of *Peperoni alla Siciliana* (page 162)

MACCHERONI AI FERRETTI CON RAGÙ
Hand-made Maccheroni with Meat Ragù

SERVES 6

6 x 50 g (2 oz) slices of beef topside

2 tablespoons chopped fresh parsley

1 garlic clove, finely chopped

120 ml (4 fl oz) olive oil

6 lamb cutlets

350 g (12 oz) loin or shoulder of pork on the bone

6 small pieces of spicy cooking sausage, preferably air-dried (such as *cacciatorino*)

1 large onion, finely chopped

2 glasses of red wine

2 kg (4½ lb) ripe tomatoes, skinned, deseeded and chopped, or 1.5 kg (3¼ lb) *polpa di pomodoro* (see page 15)

Salt and freshly ground black pepper

Freshly grated Parmesan or pecorino cheese, to serve (optional)

Everything tends to be done in a hurry nowadays but I can recommend taking the time to prepare this simple but extremely satisfying pasta dish. It is a joy to see your guests eating something unique prepared with your own hands. Customers at the Trattoria Pezzolla in Accettura, Basilicata, know that Isabella Pezzolla Romano prepares the best ragù to serve with maccheroni ai ferretti, *which is made on the premises for special occasions. Variations on this dish are made all over Southern Italy, usually for Sunday lunch. Each family uses a different pasta shape and different meat for the ragù.*

The pasta can be prepared a day or so in advance and stored in the fridge. You will need a 2 mm (size 14) knitting needle (ferretti) *to shape the pasta.*

METHOD

To make the pasta, pile the flour up in a volcano shape on a work surface (marble is best) and make a large well in the centre. Put the eggs and water in the well, keeping back a little of the water. Lightly beat the eggs and water together with a fork and then gradually mix in the flour with your hands, adding more water if necessary, to make a fairly firm dough. Don't worry if the mixture sticks to your fingers – you can remedy this by rubbing them with a little of the flour. When the mixture has formed a dough, knead it well with the palms of your hands for about 20 minutes, scraping up any dough sticking to the work surface. When the dough is very smooth, and neither too firm nor too soft, cover and leave it to rest for 20 minutes. (Some people prefer to use a

FOR THE PASTA

800 g (1¾ lb) *doppio zero*
(00) flour (see page 14)

5 eggs

About 175 ml (6 fl oz) water

machine to make the dough, although I don't think you get such a good result.)

Now cut off little pieces of the dough and roll them on the work surface with the palm of your hand into small batons about 5 mm (¼ in) in diameter. Cut them into 6–7.5 cm (2½–3 in) lengths. To shape the pasta, put a knitting needle on top of a piece of dough and roll the dough around the needle with your hand to make a noodle with a hole through the centre. Carefully slide the noodles off the knitting needle and lay them on a clean tea towel as you make them. Leave on the tea towel while you make the sauce.

Sprinkle the slices of beef with the parsley, garlic and some seasoning, then roll them up and secure each one with a wooden cocktail stick. Heat the olive oil in a large pan, add all the meat, including the beef rolls (cook in batches if necessary), and fry until browned on all sides. Add the onion and cook gently until soft. Pour in the wine and let it bubble to evaporate a little, then add the tomatoes. Cover and cook gently for a couple of hours or until the meat is tender. Remove the piece of pork and cut it into slices.

Cook the pasta in a large pan of boiling salted water (2 teaspoons salt to each litre (1¾ pints) water) for 6–8 minutes, until *al dente*. Drain well and toss with the sauce, serving the cut-up pieces of meat on top. I prefer this dish without grated cheese but it's up to you.

FEGATO AL MARSALA
Calf's Liver with Marsala

SERVES 4

**400 g (14 oz) calf's liver,
sliced into thin strips**

2 tablespoons plain flour

4 tablespoons olive oil

6 sage leaves, finely chopped

**2 tablespoons finely chopped
fresh parsley**

120 ml (4 fl oz) dry Marsala

**Salt and freshly ground black
pepper**

Judging the quality of a vintage
1939 Marsala

The Southern counterpart of fegato alla veneziana *is this liver dish, which promises all the flavours of the South. Serve with fried potatoes and lightly cooked spinach.*

METHOD

Dust the pieces of liver in the flour, shaking off any excess. Heat the oil in a large, heavy frying pan, add the liver and fry on each side for 1–2 minutes; it's important not to overcook it. Cook in batches if necessary so as not to overcrowd the pan.

Add the sage, parsley and some salt and pepper. Pour in the Marsala and stir to coat all the pieces of liver, which will become shiny and glazed. Remove from the heat and serve immediately.

ZUPPA DI SOFFRITTO
Soffritto Soup

SERVES 8–10

400 g (14 oz) pig's liver

400 g (14 oz) pig's heart

200 g (7 oz) pig's lung

**200 g (7 oz) pig's kidneys,
soaked in water for 1 hour
and then drained**

**100 g (4 oz) lard or 120 ml
(4 fl oz) olive oil**

800 g (1¾ lb) tomato passata

2 tablespoons tomato paste

**Lots of chilli powder
(according to taste)**

Salt

Bay leaves, to serve

Toasted bread, to serve

This is a must for offal lovers. Butchers in Naples used to sell the basic mixture in slices during the winter so it could be diluted with water at home to make soup. There are several regional variations, some made with lamb's pluck and some with pork. In Tuscany a version is made with chicken, called cibreo. *This Neapolitan recipe uses the lungs, heart, liver and even kidneys of freshly slaughtered pigs – worth trying if you like offal. Cooking the meat in pork lard gives the best result but it is still good if made with olive oil.*

METHOD

Cut all the meat into small chunks and fry in the lard or olive oil until brown. Add the tomato passata and tomato paste, season with chilli and salt and cook for 1 hour or until all the meat is tender and the mixture is very thick. Transfer to a container and leave to cool. It can be stored in the fridge for up to 10 days.

To serve, take a couple of tablespoons per person, dilute with hot water and add a couple of bay leaves. When the mixture is thoroughly heated through, pour on to toasted bread in individual soup bowls.

TRIPPA DI TRASTEVERE
Tripe Trastevere-style

SERVES 4

1 kg (2¼ lb) mixed tripe, cleaned but unbleached

2 tablespoons chopped fresh mint

A small pinch of ground cloves

100 g (4 oz) pecorino cheese, grated, plus extra for sprinkling

FOR THE RAGÙ

3 tablespoons olive oil

1 small onion, finely chopped

500 g (1 lb 2 oz) boned shoulder of lamb, cut into chunks

1 small glass of dry white wine

800 g (1¾ lb) tomatoes, peeled, deseeded and diced

Salt and freshly ground black pepper

Every time I see tripe in a trusted restaurant I order it immediately because, like pasta e fagioli, *it is one of those dishes by which you can measure the chef's abilities. It is a simple dish and very tasty indeed, provided you have the right sort of tripe – not bleached or precooked, so that it still has lots of flavour. Tripe and other types of offal used to be eaten by the poor, since they were the cheapest cuts of meat. Today offal is a gourmet speciality.*

In Trastevere, on the 'right' side of the Tiber in Rome, this dish is enjoyed even by people who do not usually like tripe. Da Checco il Carrettiere is the best trattoria in Rome for offal specialities.

METHOD

First make the ragù: heat the oil in a pan, add the onion and fry until softened. Add the lamb and fry until browned all over, then pour in the wine and let it bubble to evaporate. Stir in the tomatoes and simmer for an hour or so, until the meat is very tender. Season to taste.

Boil the tripe in lightly salted water for at least 1 hour or until almost tender, then drain.

Preheat the oven to 200°C, 400°F, Gas Mark 6.

Mix the tripe with the mint, cloves, cheese, ragù and some seasoning. Put it in an ovenproof dish, sprinkle with more cheese and bake for 30–40 minutes, until the cheese has formed a crust.

POLLO DI GRAZIELLA
Graziella's Chicken

SERVES 6

1 x 2 kg (4½ lb) free-range
  chicken, cut into chunks
  (including the giblets)
3 garlic cloves, chopped
2 tablespoons chopped fresh
  parsley
5 bay leaves
2 sprigs of rosemary
2 glasses of dry white wine
1 glass of extra virgin
  olive oil
1 kg (2¼ lb) potatoes, peeled
  and quartered
3 tablespoons freshly grated
  Parmesan or pecorino
  cheese
Salt and freshly ground black
  pepper

Graziella is one of the few self-taught female chefs at the head of a five-star restaurant kitchen in Italy. She learned her trade in her mother's kitchen, which was probably full of recipes from previous mothers. Graziella prepares genuine Pugliese food at Masseria San Domenico, a five-star hotel in Savelletri, where it is a rare pleasure to eat regional specialities, mostly based on the excellent local vegetables, rather than the bland international food often served in hotels. This chicken dish should ideally be cooked in a terracotta pot placed in a wood-fired oven in a sandwich of glowing coals. However, it is also excellent cooked slowly in a conventional oven at home.

METHOD

Preheat the oven to 190°C, 375°F, Gas Mark 5.

The method is quite simple. Mix all the ingredients together in a terracotta pot, cover with a lid and leave to marinate for 1 hour. Place in the oven and cook for at least 1½ hours, or until everything is tender and succulent.

NGOZZAMODDI or AZMOT
Jewish Chicken Rissoles

SERVES 4

600 g (1 lb 5 oz) skinless boneless chicken breasts

2 eggs, beaten

4 tablespoons fresh breadcumbs

A pinch of cinnamon

6 tablespoons olive oil

2 celery sticks, cut into small cubes

1 garlic clove, finely chopped

600 g (1 lb 5 oz) *polpa di pomodoro* (see page 15)

A little stock or water, if necessary

Salt and freshly ground black pepper

Many Roman dishes are borrowed from the local Jewish community. Although strict Jews have to follow at least 55 dietary rules, I didn't feel at all restricted by the two dishes I borrowed from Donatella Limentani Pavoncello, a Roman lady, a conscientious follower of her religion, and an excellent cook and cookery writer. This recipe and the one for Torzelli (see page 152) have been in her family for 400 years and particularly appealed to me for their simplicity. Donatella traditionally adds a couple of wishbones to the sauce for good luck.

METHOD

Roughly mince the chicken. Put it in a bowl and mix with the eggs, breadcrumbs, cinnamon and some salt and pepper. Use your hands to shape the mixture into 12 rissoles.

Heat the oil in a large frying pan, add the rissoles and fry for 2–3 minutes on each side, until brown. Remove from the pan and set aside. Add the celery, garlic and tomato pulp to the pan, bring to the boil and simmer for 5 minutes. Return the rissoles to the pan and cook for another 10 minutes, adding a little stock or water if the sauce thickens too much. Serve with bread.

CONIGLIO ALLA ISCHITANA
Rabbit Ischia-style

SERVES 4

6 tablespoons extra virgin olive oil

1 x 1 kg (2¼ lb) rabbit, cut into chunks

4 garlic cloves, chopped

200 ml (7 fl oz) dry white wine (preferably Ischia Bianco)

300 g (11 oz) *polpa di pomodoro* (see page 15)

6 basil leaves, chopped

The liver from the rabbit, finely chopped

Salt and freshly ground black pepper

Rabbit is usually classed as a white meat, along with chicken, turkey, etc., because, unlike its wild cousin, the hare, the meat is very pale and tender. Since it tends to become dry when roasted or grilled, Southern Italians almost always cook rabbit in a sauce, either on top of the stove or in the oven. This dish is very popular in Ischia, where many restaurants feature it on their menu.

METHOD

Heat the oil in a large pan, add the pieces of rabbit and fry until brown on all sides. Half way through browning the rabbit, add the garlic and half the white wine. When the wine has evaporated, add the remaining wine and simmer for 10 minutes. Stir in the tomato pulp and cook for about 20 minutes, until it thickens to make a lovely sauce. Add the basil leaves, liver and some seasoning and cook for about 10 minutes, adding a little water if necessary, until the rabbit is tender.

Following pages (clockwise from left): *Torzelli* (page 152); *Ngozzamoddi* (page 116); *Braciole d'Abbacchio con Carciofi* (page 100)

PICCIONI AL SUGO CON FUNGHI
Pigeon Braised with Tomatoes and Mushrooms

SERVES 4

4 pigeons, cleaned but with giblets

6 tablespoons fresh breadcrumbs

2 eggs, beaten

2 tablespoons finely chopped fresh parsley

6 tablespoons extra virgin olive oil

500 g (1 lb 2 oz) *polpa di pomodoro* **(see page 15)**

50 g (2 oz) tomato paste

20 g (¾ oz) dried porcini mushrooms, soaked in warm water for 30 minutes, then drained and chopped

Salt and freshly ground black pepper

This popular recipe comes from Basilicata, where pigeon is sometimes replaced by pheasant or other wild birds during the hunting season. It is extremely good, especially when made with woodpigeon.

METHOD

Finely chop the giblets and then mix them with the breadcrumbs, beaten eggs, parsley and some salt and pepper. Stuff the pigeons with this mixture.

Heat the oil in a large, deep pan, add the pigeons and brown on all sides. Add the tomato pulp, tomato paste and porcini. Season with salt, then cover and cook gently for about 1¼ hours or until the pigeons are tender, uncovering the pan towards the end of the cooking time. You could use the sauce to dress pasta and serve the pigeons separately; that's what they do in Basilicata.

PERNICE ALLA SARDA
Sardinian-style Partridge

SERVES 4

8 partridges, cleaned

120 ml (4 fl oz) extra virgin olive oil

4 tablespoons white wine vinegar

3 tablespoons finely chopped fresh parsley

1 tablespoon salted capers, soaked in water for 10 minutes, then drained and finely chopped

Salt

In honour of the Sardinian hunting tradition, here is a recipe for a noble bird which will surprise many game lovers. Chicken, other small birds and even eel are prepared in the same way.

METHOD

Simmer the partridges in a large pan of lightly salted water for 20 minutes. Drain the birds and cut them into quarters. Mix together the oil, vinegar, parsley, capers and some salt. Pour this mixture over the birds, cover and leave to marinate for 24 hours. Serve cold.

PESCE

fish

The regions forming the tip of Italy are surrounded by water and enjoy one of the world's most enviable supplies of fresh fish. Fishing around the entire coast-line, including Sicily and the small islands, is a tradition as ancient as history, and fish have always represented a major source of food. Sardinia, however, has long been excluded from this 'club', since this splendid island used to suffer constant invasion from all sorts of barbarians, making it safer to live inland than on the coast. Consequently the Sardinians developed a diet built almost exclu-sively around domestic and wild animals, such as sheep, rabbits, goats, pigs and all sorts of fowl and game, in which the island is very rich. However, with the advent of tourism this way of eating is gradually disappearing and the island is starting to exploit its coastline.

Ways of cooking fish vary throughout the South, depending on which ingredi-ents are available locally. Anchovies, for example, are prepared differently in Naples, Salerno, Puglia and Sicily. The best ones come from Sicily and are delicious when matured under salt for at least a year and filleted just before use. The flesh is pink and has a wonderful smell and flavour. My favourite way of eating salted anchovies is on a piece of buttered bread, while fresh ones are nicest baked briefly in the oven. Sardines also enjoy great popularity in the South. I particularly like them fried and then marinated in oil and vinegar with mint and garlic to serve as an *antipasto* (see *Sarde alla Scapece* on page 130).

Big fish such as tuna, swordfish and even shark are fished off Sicily and Cal-abria. They are cut into steaks and grilled, fried, baked or stewed like meat. Recently it has become fashionable to use such fish to make *carpaccio*, thin slices of very fresh raw fish marinated in lemon or vinegar and oil.

Previous pages: Selection of fresh fish

The array of shellfish, together with squid, octopus and fish such as sardines, scorpion fish and monkfish, forms the base of *brodetto*, a briefly cooked stew which makes an excellent main course.

Finally *baccalà*, or dried salt cod, is a major part of the diet, although it comes as a surprise in a land where so much fresh fish is available. It used to be the cheapest form of fish but not today, when it is becoming almost a delicacy. In the fish markets of Naples and Palermo you will find desalted and softened *baccalà* on sale for immediate use. People in the South love this fish, which is extremely tasty and versatile. They fry it in batter, stew it with tomatoes or boil it and serve it as a salad, dressed with good olive oil, lemon, garlic and parsley – a real treat!

Fish main courses are usually accompanied by salads if grilled, or tender vegetables if stewed. Religious customs are still observed in the South, so fish is a must for the Friday meal, but it is now eaten as a main course on other days of the week too. The high demand means that it has become quite expensive to buy fresh. However, the modern way of freezing fish for later use or buying ready-frozen fish is not something I would recommend, since the flavour of fish treated in this way changes completely, not to mention the loss of texture. I am glad to see that, although it is much cheaper, frozen fish doesn't easily enter Southern Italian kitchens. It is also reassuring to note that by law restaurants have to declare on the menu if they have used frozen fish!

BRANZINO ALLA BRACE
Charcoal-grilled Sea Bass

SERVES 4

4 x 450 g (1 lb) sea bass,
cleaned but not scaled

Extra virgin olive oil for
frying

Freshly ground black pepper
(optional)

FOR THE MARINADE

300 ml (10 fl oz) water

50 g (2 oz) sea salt

Juice of 1 lemon

2 tablespoons white wine
vinegar

2 tablespoons very finely
chopped fresh chives

In Sardinia this recipe is made with various types of scaly fish. The marinade and the scales help the flesh remain juicy and flavoursome during grilling. Originally the marinade was made with seawater but because it is difficult to find completely clean and unpolluted, it is better to use water in which you have dissolved some sea salt.

METHOD

To make the marinade, put the water and salt in a pan and boil until the salt has dissolved. Leave to cool and then add the lemon juice, vinegar and chives.

Put the fish in a dish, pour over the marinade and leave for 1 hour. Cook the fish on a charcoal grill for 10–12 minutes on each side, basting from time to time with the marinade. Skin and bone the fish, then serve with a drizzle of olive oil and a sprinkling of black pepper if desired. A very delicate fish indeed.

ZUPPA DI PESCE DI GALLIPOLI
Gallipoli Fish Soup

SERVES 4

2 kg (4½ lb) mixed fish and shellfish, such as grouper, bream, scorpion fish, squid, imperial prawns, mussels, red mullet, etc.

120 ml (4 fl oz) extra virgin olive oil

1 onion, finely sliced

600 g (1 lb 5 oz) ripe tomatoes, deseeded and cut into strips

2 tablespoons white wine vinegar

Salt and freshly ground black pepper

Slices of toasted bread, to serve

You could say, 'In every port, a new fish soup,' because there are as many versions of this soup in Italy as there are ports or coastal towns. The idea is to collect all the wonderful juices and flavours of Mediterranean fish in one pot. The fish, especially around Gallipoli, Taranto and Brindisi, are so flavoursome that there is no need to make a fish stock beforehand – they are simply added to the pot whole. Coping with all the bones may seem a little fiddly but it's worth taking the time to enjoy every little bit of a good fish soup.

METHOD

Clean and descale the fish but leave them whole. Clean the squid. Scrub the mussels thoroughly under cold running water, pulling out the beards and discarding any open mussels that do not close when tapped on a work surface.

Heat the oil in a large pan, add the onion and fry until soft. Then add the tomatoes, vinegar and a pinch of salt and pepper and simmer for 10 minutes. Put the fish in the pan, adding the ones requiring a longer cooking time first, then bring to the boil. Reduce the heat, cover and cook gently, without stirring, for 20–30 minutes until all the fish are cooked through. Season to taste and serve in bowls, with slices of toasted bread.

POLIPO AFFOGATO
Drowned Octopus

SERVES 4

1 large octopus, weighing
   1.25 kg (2½ lb)
150 ml (5 fl oz) olive oil
1 large garlic clove, coarsely
   chopped
¼ medium chilli, finely
   chopped
150 ml (5 fl oz) dry white
   wine
250 g (9 oz) ripe tomatoes,
   finely chopped
2 tablespoons coarsely
   chopped fresh parsley
Salt and freshly ground black
   pepper

This is a common way of cooking octopus in the South. The gentle heat and long simmering makes it very tender indeed. Sometimes no liquid at all is added and the octopus simply stews in its own juices. This recipe works best with a small octopus, cooked in a covered terracotta pot. Fishermen drink the resulting liquid for medicinal purposes. It is, however, wonderful mopped up with bread.

METHOD

Clean the octopus, leaving it whole – do not cut any part of it. Gently heat the olive oil in a pan in which the octopus will just fit. Add the garlic and chilli and fry briefly without letting them burn. Pick up the octopus by its head and dip it into the pan a few times to make it curl up. Put it in the pan, raise the heat and cook for 3–5 minutes. Add the wine and boil until it has reduced by half its volume. Then stir in the tomatoes and parsley and season with salt and pepper. Cover the pan and cook over the lowest possible heat for 1¼ hours, stirring from time to time, until the octopus is tender.

Typical varieties of fresh fish from Palermo:

(clockwise from top left) grey mullet,

prawns, squid, baby octopus, cuttlefish,

cicerielli (baby eel)

SARDE ALLA SCAPECE
Marinated Fried Sardines

SERVES 4

1 kg (2¼ lb) fresh sardines, cleaned

Plain flour for dusting

100 ml (3½ fl oz) olive oil, plus extra for shallow-frying

1 garlic clove, finely sliced

6 tablespoons white wine vinegar

120 ml (4 fl oz) dry white wine

3 tablespoons finely chopped fresh mint

Salt and freshly ground black pepper

This method of marinating fried fish and serving it cold is popular throughout the South. Many different fish can be used, such as anchovies, mackerel and sardines. It makes an ideal summer antipasto or main course.

METHOD

Dust the sardines in flour, shaking off any excess, then fry them in plenty of hot olive oil until they are crisp and brown. Transfer to a shallow dish.

In a separate pan, heat the 100 ml (3½ fl oz) olive oil and fry the garlic in it very briefly. Add the vinegar, wine and mint, then remove from the heat. While it is still hot, pour this mixture over the fish. Season to taste and leave to marinate for a couple of hours before serving.

SOGLIOLE GRATINATE
Baked Sole with Parmesan

SERVES 4

4 x 300 g (11 oz) Dover sole, cleaned, skinned and fins trimmed

8 tablespoons dried breadcrumbs

1 garlic clove, very finely chopped

4 tablespoons finely chopped fresh parsley

6 tablespoons grated pecorino cheese

6 tablespoons olive oil

Salt and freshly ground black pepper

Any dish baked in the oven comes as a relief to those who do not like standing over a hot stove. The only work involved in this recipe is the easy preparation of the fish. The result, as is often the case with simple dishes made from good-quality ingredients, is stunning. The combination of herbs and cheese with fish is very interesting.

METHOD

Preheat the oven to 220°C, 425°F, Gas Mark 7.

With a very sharp knife, make an incision right down the centre of each fish to reach the bone. Season the fish with salt and pepper and put them on a baking sheet. Mix the dried breadcrumbs with the garlic and parsley and spread on both sides of the incision, using a spatula. Sprinkle the cheese down the centre, then drizzle the olive oil all over the fish. Bake in the oven for 15 minutes, until the fish are tender.

Following pages (from left):

Sarde alla Scapece (page 130);

Sogliole Gratinate (above)

BACCALÀ ALLA NAPOLETANA
Salt Cod Neapolitan-style

SERVES 4

8 x 120 g (4½ oz) fillets of
baccalà

Plain flour for dusting

Olive oil for shallow-frying

1 garlic clove, finely chopped

500 g (1 lb 2 oz) polpa di
pomodoro (see page 15) or
600 g (1 lb 5 oz) fresh
tomatoes, finely chopped

1 tablespoon salted capers,
soaked in water for
10 minutes, then drained

2 tablespoons black olives,
pitted

1 tablespoon raisins

1 tablespoon pine kernels

Freshly ground black pepper

Despite all the impeccably fresh fish available in the Bay of Naples, you will find plenty of Neapolitans who love preserved fish. Baccalà, or dried salt cod, used to be a very economical way of eating fish. Now that it is not particularly cheap any more it is eaten for nostalgia's sake and for its highly distinctive flavour. In Naples you can buy baccalà *ready desalted and softened for immediate use, which cuts out the lengthy soaking process.*

METHOD

Soak the salt cod in cold water for at least 24 hours, until softened, changing the water 3 or 4 times.

Drain the cod and pat dry, then dust it with flour, shaking off any excess. Heat some olive oil in a pan, add the pieces of cod and fry for 4–5 minutes on each side, until golden. Remove from the pan and set aside. Add the garlic to the pan and fry gently for 1 minute, then add the tomato pulp, capers, olives, raisins and pine kernels and some black pepper. Bring to a simmer, then return the fish to the pan, reduce the heat and cook gently, uncovered, for 15 minutes.

TONNO CON PISELLI
Tuna with Peas

SERVES 4

6 tablespoons olive oil

2 garlic cloves, finely chopped

2 tablespoons coarsely chopped fresh flat-leaf parsley

800 g (1¾ lb) tuna, cut into 4 steaks

500 g (1 lb 2 oz) *polpa di pomodoro* (see page 15)

300 g (11 oz) fresh peas, (shelled weight)

Salt and freshly ground black pepper

An extremely simple Sicilian recipe using fresh tuna, which when in season is abundant around the entire Southern coast. It takes only a short time to cook.

Very fresh and tender garden peas give the best results. You could use frozen peas, but there will inevitably be a loss of flavour.

METHOD

Heat the oil in a large heavy frying pan and add the garlic and parsley, then immediately add the tuna steaks. Fry briefly, then turn the steaks over. By this time the garlic will have started to brown. Season with salt and pepper, add the tomato pulp and cook for 5 minutes. Remove the tuna steaks from the pan and set aside. Add the peas to the tomato sauce and cook gently until tender. Return the tuna to the pan, heat through and serve.

RAGÙ DI TONNO
Tuna Ragù

SERVES 6

A nice piece of fresh tuna, weighing 1.25 kg (2½ lb)

3 garlic cloves, cut into slivers

A few sprigs of mint

6 tablespoons olive oil

1 onion, finely sliced

4 anchovy fillets, chopped

1 tablespoon salted capers, soaked in water for 10 minutes, then drained

1 kg (2¼ lb) *polpa di pomodoro* (see page 15)

Salt and freshly ground black pepper

This recipe is from Sicily, where tuna is cooked in many different ways. You can serve it with pasta, tossing the pasta with the tomato sauce and then eating the tuna afterwards as a main course. The tuna can also be eaten cold, which makes it easier to slice.

METHOD

With a small, sharp knife, make a few incisions in the tuna and insert the garlic slivers and sprigs of mint. Tie with string to keep the tuna in shape.

Heat the olive oil in a large pan and fry the tuna on a high heat just until browned on both sides. Reduce the heat, add the onion and fry until soft, then add the anchovy fillets and capers. Stir in the tomato pulp and cook gently for 20–30 minutes, until the tomatoes have formed a sauce and the fish is cooked through. Season to taste, then remove the piece of tuna, cut off the string and slice the fish. Serve with the sauce.

PESCE SPADA AGGHIOTTA
Swordfish with Tomato Sauce

SERVES 4

120 ml (4 fl oz) extra virgin
olive oil

1 small onion, finely chopped

1 tablespoon salted capers,
soaked in water for
10 minutes, then drained

2 tablespoons green olives,
pitted and chopped

4 x 165 g (5½ oz) slices of
swordfish

1 tablespoon chopped fresh
parsley

1 tablespoon chopped fresh
basil

1 small glass of dry white
wine

600 g (1 lb 5 oz) tomatoes,
chopped

Salt and freshly ground black
pepper

In the charming village of Scilla in the channel of Messina, the fishermen make a living from fishing for swordfish, which, they claim, gather from all over the Mediterranean Sea to mate in the picturesque bay. The unfortunate 'lovers' are often caught in pairs, destined for the pots and pans of local restaurants. A tragic end to delight the palates of many.

METHOD

Heat the oil in a large pan and briefly fry the onion until softened. Add the capers and olives and cook, stirring, for a couple of minutes. Add the swordfish and fry for a few minutes on each side, until browned. Stir in the parsley, basil and some seasoning, then pour in the wine and let it bubble until most of it has evaporated. Add the tomatoes, lower the heat and cook for 10 minutes, until the sauce has thickened. Adjust the seasoning and serve.

INVOLTINI DI PESCE SPADA
Swordfish Rolls

SERVES 4

75 g (3 oz) stale bread

6 tablespoons olive oil

25 g (1 oz) Parmesan cheese,
   cut into very small cubes

50 g (2 oz) provola cheese,
   cut into very small cubes

1 tablespoon salted capers,
   soaked in water for
   10 minutes, then drained
   and finely chopped

2 tablespoons chopped fresh
   parsley

8 slices of swordfish
   (preferably cut from the
   belly), about 5 mm (¼ in)
   thick

15 g (½ oz) butter, cut into
   8 small strips

Juice of 1 lemon

Salt and freshly ground black
   pepper

No one knows who invented this recipe, although both Sicilians and Calabrians claim the rights to it. It doesn't matter to us; we can just enjoy this simple dish.

METHOD

To make the filling, crumble the bread into a bowl, add 1 tablespoon of the oil and 1 tablespoon of water and mix together with your hands to loosen the bread. Then add the cheeses, capers, half the parsley and some salt and pepper. Mix together to form a soft dough.

Put the swordfish slices on a work surface and place a piece of the filling rolled into a sausage shape on top of each one. Place a strip of butter on the filling and roll up the fish. Secure with wooden cocktail sticks.

Heat the remaining oil in a large pan and fry the rolls for 2 minutes on each side. Sprinkle with the lemon juice and the remaining parsley and serve with some of the cooking juices poured over.

TONNO AL FORNO CON SALMORIGLIO
Baked Tuna with Herbs

SERVES 4

4 x 200 g (7 oz) fresh tuna steaks

2 tablespoons pine kernels

2 tablespoons dried breadcrumbs

FOR THE SALMORIGLIO

4 garlic cloves, chopped

3 tablespoons very finely chopped fresh mint

3 tablespoons very finely chopped fresh parsley

2 tablespoons salted capers, soaked in water for 10 minutes, then drained

Juice and grated rind of 2 lemons

1 teaspoon dried wild oregano

Extra virgin olive oil

Salt and freshly ground black pepper

It is a joy to shop in the Vucceria market of Palermo. The fish is so fresh and so appetizingly displayed that it is impossible to resist. Fresh tuna is now available everywhere, often replacing meat because it does not have a noticeably fishy taste. For this recipe you could substitute swordfish or any large fish that can be cut into thick slices. Tuna, however, is perfect, and the aristocratic guests I cooked it for in Palermo were most enthusiastic about my interpretation of Sicilian cooking. They were intrigued to see that the salmoriglio, *a mixture of herbs generally used to dress steamed or grilled fish, was cooked with the fish in this case.*

METHOD

Preheat the oven to 220°C, 425°F, Gas Mark 7.

To make the *salmoriglio*, put the chopped garlic in a mortar and pound it to a fine pulp. Add the mint, parsley, capers, lemon juice and rind, oregano and enough olive oil to make an almost liquid mixture. Pound together to make a thick sauce, then season with salt and pepper.

Season the tuna steaks, place them on an oiled baking tray and spread the *salmoriglio* over them. Sprinkle the breadcrumbs and pine kernels on top and bake for 6–7 minutes, until the tuna is just cooked through.

Following pages (from left): *Tonno al Forno con Salmoriglio* (above); *Involtini di Pesce Spada* (page 138)

ANGUILLA ALLA ROMANA
Eel Roman-style

SERVES 4

800 g (1¾ lb) eel, gutted and
cut into 7.5 cm (3 in) chunks

Plain flour for dusting

6 tablespoons extra virgin
olive oil

2 garlic cloves, very finely
chopped

½ chilli, very finely chopped

2 tablespoons salted capers,
soaked in water for
10 minutes, then drained

4 anchovy fillets, chopped

1 glass of dry white wine

2 tablespoons mint leaves

The Romans love eel, especially at Christmas when they cook the capitone, *a very large eel which is grilled and then marinated. The recipe below includes mint, which is used a lot in Roman cooking.*

METHOD

Dust the eel chunks in flour, shaking off any excess, then fry in the olive oil for 4 minutes on each side, until tender. Remove from the pan and set aside.

Add the garlic, chilli, capers and anchovies to the pan. As soon as the garlic begins to brown, add the wine and let it bubble for a minute or two over a high heat to allow it to evaporate a little. Return the eel to the pan together with the mint, reduce the heat and cook for another 2 minutes. Serve immediately.

ARAGOSTA AL FORNO
Baked Lobster

SERVES 4

**4 x 500g (1lb 2oz) live
  lobsters**

6 tablespoons virgin olive oil

**4 tablespoons very finely
  chopped fresh parsley**

Juice of 1 lemon

**Salt and freshly ground black
  pepper**

When you have a relative abundance of lobsters and you want to enjoy them prepared simply, as fishermen do in Sardinia, then you don't need to look for sophisticated ways of cooking the king of crustacea.

METHOD

Preheat the oven to 200°C, 400°F, Gas mark 6. Cut the live lobsters in half. (If you pierce through the cross mark in the centre of the head they will be killed instantly.) Mix the other ingredients together and pour them over the lobster flesh. Bake for 20–25 minutes, then serve with more lemon juice if desired. It's as simple as that!

VEGETABLES
vegetables and

E CONTORNI
accompaniments

Vegetables play one of the most important roles in the Mediterranean diet, especially in the South of Italy where they are eaten raw, roasted, grilled, fried, stewed or preserved. They can be served as an *antipasto*, a first course, an accompaniment to meat or fish, or even as a main course. Vegetable desserts are not unknown either. *Melanzane e Cioccolato* (see page 184) is a delicious speciality from the Amalfi coast, consisting of boiled aubergine slices that have been dipped in egg and fried, sandwiched together with candied peel and egged and fried again, then served with chocolate sauce poured over.

The vegetables available in shops and markets are almost exclusively cultivated locally and eaten seasonally, which means that quality and flavour are at a peak while prices are at their lowest. Everyone looks forward to special vegetables such as asparagus, artichokes, broad beans and fennel coming into season. It's a very different story from those unfortunate countries where the same produce is available the entire year round, specially flown in from the most remote corners of the world and virtually devoid of flavour. I don't see any point in eating a huge tomato, grown in a greenhouse, perfect in colour and shape, but completely tasteless. There is no comparison with those perfumed fruits of the South, freshly picked from a plant that has grown outdoors, where it has enjoyed all the sun in the world and the meticulous care of the farmer.

Spring is the best time to taste the *primizie*, the first tender produce to appear on the market. These include bunches of spring onions, asparagus, fresh broad beans (mostly eaten raw with pecorino cheese) and artichokes, which can be eaten raw in salads when very young and tender, or cooked in numerous ways. The artichoke, incidentally, is cultivated everywhere and is loved with the same

Previous pages: Selection of fresh vegetables

intensity in every region of the South. Springtime, starting from March in the South, also offers a great variety of wild foods, such as dandelion, wild fennel, wild asparagus and rocket. These are picked by local people and brought from the countryside to the city, where they are presented in immaculately tied bunches and sold (not cheaply) to all those who don't have the opportunity to gather them for themselves. These wild greens with their intense flavours make the tastiest of salads and can also be used for hearty soups or *minestre* (vegetable stews).

It is inspirational to observe how Southern Italians treat all vegetables as delicacies, which with just a few touches and the appropriate flavouring can be turned into delicious specialities. The shoots of simple wild hops, gathered in waste areas, taste so nutty and delicious that they can be eaten as a sophisticated vegetable dish or even *pasticciati* (stirred) with scrambled eggs.

A great deal of preserving is undertaken in Southern Italy, using the pick of the season's produce to capture the full flavour. Tomatoes are bottled in their own juices, making an excellent base for sauces in the winter months. An interesting way of preserving a combination of vegetables, such as aubergines, small artichokes, onions and peppers, is to pickle them with olives and capers in a mixture called *giardiniera*, which is served as an *antipasto*.

CAPONATA DI VERDURE
Vegetable Caponata

SERVES 6

150 ml (5 fl oz) olive oil

50 g (2 oz) dried
  breadcrumbs

200 g (7 oz) cauliflower
  florets

3 heads of chicory, cut in half

200 g (7 oz) celery sticks, cut
  into chunks

200 g (7 oz) cardoons (the
  tender centre part only), cut
  into chunks (optional)

300 g (11 oz) fresh spinach

200 g (7 oz) curly endive
  (frisé)

2 tablespoons white wine
  vinegar

1 tablespoon salted capers,
  soaked in water for
  10 minutes, then drained

8 anchovy fillets

Salt and freshly ground black
  pepper

This is an alternative version of the famous Sicilian caponata di melanzane, *which is based on aubergines. Many more vegetables are included here, resulting in an excellent dish.*

METHOD

Heat 2 tablespoons of the olive oil in a small pan, add the breadcrumbs and fry until browned. Remove from the heat and set aside.

Cook all the vegetables separately in a large pan of lightly salted boiling water until just tender, then drain well. Heat the remaining olive oil in a large frying pan (or, better, a wok), add the cooked vegetables and stir-fry for 1–2 minutes until well mixed. Stir in the vinegar and some seasoning and mix well again. Place on a serving dish and sprinkle over the breadcrumbs and capers, then garnish with the anchovies. Serve warm or cold, as an *antipasto* or a side dish.

FAVE AL GUANCIALE
Broad Beans
with Pork Cheek

SERVES 4

120 ml (4 fl oz) virgin olive oil

100 g (4 oz) *guanciale* (see page 16) or air-cured streaky bacon, cut into small strips

1 large onion, finely sliced

1.5 kg (3¼ lb) fresh young broad beans, shelled

Salt and freshly ground black pepper

Campo dei Fiori is a famous Roman square where a market is held daily. There the Romans are spoiled for choice. All kinds of seasonal fruit and vegetables are so appetizingly exhibited and loudly praised that you cannot resist buying. When I visited the market the broad beans were beautifully green and shiny, a reliable indication that they were perfectly fresh and tender. Guanciale (see page 16) is used in many dishes from Lazio.

METHOD

Heat the oil in a pan and fry the *guanciale* until it has browned. Lower the heat, add the onion and fry until softened. Add the broad beans, then pour in enough water just to cover them. Cover the pan and braise for about 20 minutes, until the beans are tender, adding more water if necessary. Season to taste and serve. This is eaten either with bread or as an accompaniment to pork and lamb.

FAVE E CICORIE ('NCAPRIATA)
Broad Beans and Chicory

SERVES 4

400 g (14 oz) skinless dried broad beans, soaked in cold water overnight

1 potato, peeled and sliced

1 celery stick

1 ripe tomato

1 small onion, peeled

2 garlic cloves, peeled

600 g (1 lb 5 oz) chicory

Salt and freshly ground black pepper

Extra virgin olive oil, to serve

This is a peasant dish from Puglia, which I sampled in Lecce at a restaurant owned by Tonio Piceci – a gourmet who shares my passion for preserving regional food and features authentic local dishes on his menu. It is important to use the best-quality ingredients, such as really good olive oil and dried broad beans. In Puglia, the chicory used would be catalogna puntarelle, *which is very similar to dandelions. Wild dandelions can be substituted for the chicory when in season, or you could use curly endive.*

This is eaten as a first course and is very filling.

METHOD

Drain the broad beans, put them in a pan and cover with fresh water. Add the potato, celery stick, tomato, onion and garlic cloves. Bring to the boil and simmer for 1 hour or until the beans are very tender. Discard the celery, tomato, onion and garlic – the potato will have disintegrated by now. Over a low heat, whisk the beans to a thick purée, adding a little hot water if necessary. Season to taste with salt and pepper and then set aside.

Cook the chicory in boiling salted water until just tender and then drain well. Serve the bean purée topped with the chicory and drizzled with abundant extra virgin olive oil.

BARBA DI FRATE SALTATA
Friar's Beard Sauté

SERVES 4

800 g (1¾ lb) *barba di frate*

120 ml (4 fl oz) extra virgin olive oil

2 garlic cloves, chopped

1 chilli, finely chopped, including the seeds

Juice of 1 lemon

Salt

To accompany Fave al Guanciale *(see page 149), I found in the Campo dei Fiori market in Rome a vegetable called* barba di frate, *or friar's beard, because of its appearance. In fact the small plants, which can be eaten raw or cooked, look like chives and taste slightly sour. Broccoli, dandelions or rape tops can all be substituted for the friar's beard in this recipe.*

METHOD

Blanch the *barba di frate* in lightly salted boiling water for 1–2 minutes, then drain well. Heat the oil in a pan, add the garlic and chilli and fry briefly without letting the garlic brown. Add the *barba di frate* and cook for 2–3 minutes, stirring, until coated in the oil. Serve hot or cold, sprinkled with the lemon juice and salt to taste.

ZUCCHINI AL POMODORO E BASILICO
Courgettes with Tomato and Basil

SERVES 4

800 g (1¾ lb) courgettes

6 tablespoons virgin olive oil

2 garlic cloves, coarsely chopped

800 g (1¾ lb) ripe tomatoes, skinned, deseeded and chopped

1 bunch of basil, chopped

Salt

This extremely easy dish from Sicily makes a good accompaniment to fish and white meat. Choose small, firm courgettes.

METHOD

Cut the courgettes into cubes and set aside. Heat the oil in a large pan, add the garlic and fry briefly. Stir in the tomatoes, basil and courgettes, then cover and cook gently for 15–18 minutes, until all the courgettes are tender. Season with salt and serve hot or cold.

TORZELLI
Fried Curly Endive

SERVES 4

4 large heads of curly endive (frisé) or 8 small ones

Extra virgin olive oil for frying

Salt and freshly ground black pepper

This recipe was given to me by Donatella Limentani Pavoncello, from her family collection of Roman Jewish recipes. It is so simple and makes a good accompaniment to Ngozzamoddi *(see page 116).*

METHOD

Discard the tough, dark green outer leaves of the curly endive, leaving just the tender ones on the stalk. Cook for 2 minutes in lightly salted boiling water, then drain well and pat dry. Fry the leaves one by one in olive oil over a moderately high heat, turning them until brown and crisp all over. Sprinkle with salt and pepper. Serve hot or cold.

ZUCCHINI A CACIO E UOVA
Egg and Cheese Courgettes

SERVES 4

120 ml (4 fl oz) virgin olive oil

1 small onion, finely chopped

2 garlic cloves, peeled but left whole

1 kg (2¼ lb) courgettes, thinly sliced

4 eggs, beaten

75 g (3 oz) Parmesan or pecorino cheese, freshly grated

2 tablespoons finely chopped fresh basil leaves

Salt and freshly ground black pepper

The expression a cacio e uova *is quite common in Southern Italian cooking. Cheese and eggs are ingredients that everyone can buy and the combination is often added to vegetable dishes. This recipe is not to be confused with a* frittata; *it is a loose mixture, rather like scrambled eggs. Simple to prepare, and extremely refreshing for the body, it is usually eaten with bread as a first course.*

METHOD

Heat the oil in a saucepan and gently fry the onion and garlic until softened. Discard the garlic, then add the courgettes, 3 tablespoons of hot water and some seasoning. Cook on a moderate heat for 15 minutes, until the courgettes are tender.

In a bowl, mix together the eggs, cheese and basil. Season to taste and pour on to the courgettes. Cook gently, stirring with a wooden spoon, to obtain a soft mixture and then serve with some fresh bread.

INSALATA DI ARANCE E LIMONI
Salad of Oranges and Lemons

SERVES 4

4 oranges, preferably blood oranges

4 lemons (not too sour) or 2 grapefruit

Juice of 1 lime

4 tablespoons extra virgin olive oil

Salt and freshly ground black pepper

Sprigs of mint, to garnish

For maximum flavour, this refreshing salad should be made with ripe, perfumed fruit. I was lucky enough to be able to pick fruit straight from the tree in an orange and lemon grove in Calabria. Southern Italian lemons are not as sour as ordinary ones. Unfortunately they are difficult to find outside Italy but you could use grapefruit instead.

METHOD

Peel the oranges, removing all the white pith. Hold each orange in your hand and, with a small sharp knife, cut out each segment from between the membranes. Peel the lemons or grapefruit, removing all the pith, and slice them thinly.

Put the fruit in a ceramic bowl. Whisk together the lime juice, olive oil and some salt and pour this dressing over the fruit. Grind over some black pepper, garnish with mint sprigs and serve. Excellent with cold meat or roasts.

CIPOLLE ALLA DON PIPPO
Stuffed Onions Don Pippo

SERVES 4

8 large onions, preferably red and sweet

200 g (7 oz) fresh breadcrumbs, softened in water, then squeezed dry

1 tablespoon finely chopped fresh basil

1 tablespoon finely chopped fresh parsley

75 g (3 oz) pecorino cheese, cut into small cubes

75 g (3 oz) pecorino or Parmesan cheese, grated

1 tablespoon salted capers, soaked in water for 10 minutes, then drained and roughly chopped

2 eggs, beaten

120 ml (4 fl oz) olive oil

2 tablespoons dried breadcrumbs

Salt and freshly ground black pepper

Following pages (from left): *Cipolle alla Don Pippo* (above); *Insalata di Arance e Limoni* (page 154)

The red Tropea onion has a mild, sweet flavour and is usually eaten raw in salads (see Insalata di Cipolle di Tropea *on page 165). It is grown in Calabria, particularly in the area round the Capo Vaticano, a promontory on which stands the Tropea lighthouse. This recipe is dedicated to Pippo Benedetto, who has been the lighthouse keeper there for 32 years and has become a sort of local legend. When I cooked for him the look on his face was enough to convince me that he liked this new way of using onions. You can, of course, substitute other types of onion.*

METHOD

Preheat the oven to 200°C, 400°F, Gas Mark 6.

Peel the onions and cut the top off each one. With a sharp knife, remove the inside of each onion, leaving a shell about 1 cm (½ in) thick.

Mix together the fresh breadcrumbs, basil, parsley, cubed pecorino, grated cheese, capers, eggs and 2 tablespoons of the olive oil. Season with salt and pepper to taste, then stuff the onions with this mixture. Put them in an ovenproof dish, dust with the dried breadcrumbs and drizzle over the remaining olive oil. Bake for 30 minutes, until the onions are tender.

PATATE IN TEGAME AL FORNO
Baked Potatoes Calabrese-style

SERVES 6

1.5 kg (3¼ lb) potatoes, peeled and sliced, but not too thinly

600 g (1 lb 5 oz) large, meaty, ripe tomatoes, sliced

20 fresh basil leaves

120 g (4½ oz) fresh (*dolce*) pecorino cheese, grated

50 g (2 oz) dried breadcrumbs

120 ml (4 fl oz) extra virgin olive oil

Salt and freshly ground black pepper

Although potatoes are widely used in Southern Italy, they are not a substitute for bread or pasta. Instead they are treated as a vegetable – served on their own or as an accompaniment to meat or fish. The best results for this recipe are obtained if you use a tiano *(terracotta pot) and cook the potatoes in a wood-fired oven. But who today possesses such a 'luxury'? A deep baking dish and a conventional oven will do.*

METHOD

Preheat the oven to 200°C, 400°F, Gas Mark 6.

In an ovenproof dish (preferably terracotta) build layers of potato, tomato and basil, sprinkling salt and pepper and grated pecorino cheese over each layer. Sprinkle the breadcrumbs over the top and pour over the olive oil. Add a little water and then bake for about 40 minutes, until the potatoes are tender.

FUNGHI MISTI ALLA BRACE
Charcoal-grilled Wild Mushrooms

SERVES 4

800 g (1¾ lb) mixed wild mushrooms (or cultivated ones)

150 ml (5 fl oz) extra virgin olive oil

Juice of ½ lemon

3 tablespoons very finely chopped fresh parsley

1 chilli, very finely chopped

1 garlic clove, very finely chopped

Salt and freshly ground black pepper

If you are served grilled mushrooms in Italy they will usually be large porcini. However, during the mushroom season a variety of both wild and cultivated mushrooms may be used, resulting in an interesting mixture of textures, colours and flavours. This dish is a real delicacy, and ideal for vegetarians. In the South, and particularly in Puglia, the most popular mushroom is the cardoncello, *a kind of very meaty oyster mushroom.*

METHOD

Thoroughly clean the mushrooms and cut any thick ones in half. Mix together the olive oil, lemon juice, parsley, chilli and garlic. Brush this mixture all over the mushrooms. Place the mushrooms on a charcoal grill and cook for just a few minutes if they are small or longer for larger ones. Season with salt and pepper and serve immediately, either alone or as an accompaniment to grilled meat.

Following pages:

Funghi Misti alla Brace (above)

PEPERONI ALLA SICILIANA
Peppers Sicilian-style

SERVES 4

6 tablespoons virgin olive oil

800 g (1¾ lb) mixed red and yellow peppers, deseeded and cut into thin strips

6 garlic cloves, peeled but left whole

100 g (4 oz) mixed black and green olives

2 tablespoons salted capers, soaked in water for 10 minutes, then drained

6 anchovy fillets

3 tablespoons white wine vinegar

Salt

For this dish you need fleshy red and yellow peppers, which in Sicily have a very sweet, intense flavour. Serve it as an accompaniment to Scaloppine al Marsala Secco (see page 105), pork escalopes or even stuffed lamb.

METHOD

Put the oil, peppers and garlic cloves in a large, heavy-based pan and cook over a fairly high heat for 10 minutes, stirring often to prevent burning. Add the olives and capers and continue to cook over a high heat, stirring, until the peppers begin to soften. Add the anchovy fillets, stirring until they dissolve. Add the vinegar and stir for a few minutes to allow the flavours to blend. Season with salt. Delicious eaten hot or cold.

PEPOLATA
Red Pepper and Anchovy Sauce

SERVES 4–6

4 red peppers

**4 teaspoons salted capers,
soaked in water for
10 minutes, then drained**

1 garlic clove, chopped

2 chillies, chopped

20 anchovy fillets

**About 150 ml (5 fl oz) extra
virgin olive oil**

While filming the television series that accompanies this book, we visited the church of San Lorenzo in Sogliano Cavour. Lorenzo died a martyr on the grill. His saint's day is still celebrated and, as part of the festivities, I cooked fresh sausages (see page 103) for ten local people called Lorenzo. After all, what could be more appropriate than a grilled dish? I felt the sausages needed an accompaniment so I devised this sauce. It is delicious with all sorts of grilled food and also with boiled meat and fish. The name is a cross between peperonata *and* gremolata, *one a dish of braised peppers and tomatoes and the other a sauce to go with all sorts of dishes. To change the colour you could use yellow peppers instead of red ones.*

METHOD

Roast the red peppers under a hot grill until blackened and blistered all over, then leave to cool. Remove the skin and seeds.

Put the peppers in a blender with the capers, garlic, chillies and anchovies and add enough olive oil to make a smooth but not too liquid sauce. Serve as an accompaniment to grilled food.

POLPETTE DI MELANZANE
Aubergine Rissoles

SERVES 4–6

1.5 kg (3¼ lb) aubergines

4 eggs, beaten

2 tablespoons finely chopped fresh parsley

1 garlic clove, extremely finely chopped

75 g (3 oz) aged pecorino cheese (or Parmesan cheese), grated

A few tablespoons dried breadcrumbs

Olive oil for frying

Salt and freshly ground black pepper

This is an authentic Pugliese dish, easy to make and quite irresistible. Different versions of this recipe crop up here and there but this is by far the best.

METHOD

Cut off the aubergine stalks and boil the aubergines in lightly salted water until soft. Drain and leave to cool, then squeeze out all the water. Purée the aubergines in a food processor or, better, chop them very finely by hand. Put the pulp in a bowl and mix in the beaten eggs, parsley, garlic, cheese and some seasoning. Add enough breadcrumbs to give a soft, workable mixture. With your hands, shape the mixture into small rissoles, about 5 cm (2 in) in diameter.

Heat some olive oil in a large frying pan and fry the rissoles until brown on both sides. Excellent hot or cold.

INSALATA DI CIPOLLE DI TROPEA
Tropea Onion Salad

SERVES 4

2 sweet onions, thickly sliced

1 celery heart

200 g (7 oz) pitted large
   green olives

400 g (14 oz) cherry
   tomatoes

6 tablespoons virgin olive oil

3 tablespoons red wine
   vinegar

1 tablespoon good-quality
   dried wild oregano

Salt and freshly ground black
   pepper

Tropea onions from Calabria have a very mild flavour and are usually eaten raw, cut into chunks and sprinkled with olive oil and vinegar. I also use them to make this salad. They are hard to find outside Italy but you could use any sweet, mild onions for this dish. Serve it on its own or, if you like, enrich it with canned tuna and hard-boiled eggs.

METHOD

Cut the celery heart into chunks. Put the onions, celery, olives and tomatoes in a bowl. Drizzle over the oil and vinegar, then sprinkle with the oregano and some salt and pepper. Mix well.

ASPARAGI SELVATICI ALL'OLIO E LIMONE
Wild Asparagus with Oil and Lemon

Should you be lucky enough to find wild asparagus, usually available in May, one way to enjoy it is simply to boil it in lightly salted water, then drain and serve with extra virgin olive oil, a drizzle of lemon juice and a sprinkling of freshly ground black pepper. You can eat it with your fingers as an appetizer or serve it as an accompaniment to meat.

POMODORI RIPIENI DI RISO
Baked Tomatoes Stuffed with Rice

SERVES 4

200 g (7 oz) risotto rice

8 large, ripe tomatoes

120 ml (4 fl oz) olive oil, plus extra for drizzling

20 mint leaves, finely chopped

1 garlic clove, finely chopped

8 anchovy fillets, finely chopped

Salt and freshly ground black pepper

The most common stuffings for vegetables are breadcrumbs, meat and tuna but in Rome tomatoes are stuffed with raw rice, which cooks in the moisture from the tomatoes. However, this depends on using very large, firm tomatoes of a type not easily available outside Italy. So here I recommend that you boil the rice briefly first.

The tomatoes can be eaten as part of an antipasto *or as a first course. My mother used to make them for a first course, as another way of serving rice.*

METHOD

Preheat the oven to 180°C, 350°F, Gas Mark 4.

Cook the rice in boiling salted water for just 5 minutes and then drain. Cut the top off each tomato but do not detach (this serves as a lid). Carefully scoop out the insides of the tomatoes, discard the seeds and chop the remaining pulp very finely. Put this in a bowl with the rice and stir in the oil, mint, garlic, anchovies and some seasoning. Fill each tomato with this mixture and cover with the 'lids'. Drizzle a little olive oil over the top and bake for 30 minutes. Serve hot, warm or cold.

FAGIOLI ALLA CAFONA
Peasant-style Beans

SERVES 4

300 g (11 oz) fresh cannellini beans (or use 200 g (7 oz) dried beans, soaked overnight, then drained)

2 ripe tomatoes, diced

1 celery stick, finely chopped

1 garlic clove, finely chopped

½ teaspoon dried oregano

½ chilli, finely chopped

6 tablespoons extra virgin olive oil

4 large slices of toasted country bread

Salt

I have finally found an Italian equivalent to beans on toast, but more interesting. Cafone *is a derogatory word for peasant, and I must say if they came up with a recipe like this they must have been gourmet peasants. This dish is typical of the province of Caserta in Campania.*

METHOD

Put the cannellini beans in a large pan with enough water to cover, then bring to the boil and simmer for 1 hour or until just tender. Add the tomatoes, celery, garlic, oregano, chilli and oil and cook for 40 minutes or until the beans are soft. Add salt to taste and serve the soupy mixture on a slice of toasted bread in individual bowls. Drizzle some extra olive oil over, if liked.

DOLCI desserts

Fruit is often eaten at the end of a meal as a simple and refreshing dessert. Southern Italians are spoiled for choice in this respect. Every region grows a wide variety of fruit in season, which is picked only when perfectly ripe, then taken to market for sale on the same day. Second-class fruit is never sold at these markets – only the best is available. Fruits such as peaches, plums, cherries, pears, figs, oranges and tangerines are tree ripened, giving them an incomparable flavour. Some fruits are made into *crostate di frutta* – shortcrust pastry tarts filled with fresh fruit and then baked – while others are turned into preserves for the winter, especially quinces and tangerines.

Nuts feature a great deal in desserts, especially in Sicily, where locally grown almonds are made into marzipan for the production of *Frutta di Martorana* (see page 178), *cassata* or elaborate moulds such as *agnello pasquale*, which is in the shape of a lamb to celebrate Easter. Hazelnuts and almonds are both used to make *croccante di nocciole*. This assembly of melted sugar, honey and nuts is a traditional Neapolitan Christmas speciality that has now spread all over the South. The other famous speciality is *torrone* (nougat), made with nuts, honey, sugar and egg white. Walnuts can be used to stuff dried figs, which are then dipped in melted bitter chocolate for a superb sweetmeat.

The culinary influence of the Arab occupations, especially in Sicily and Puglia, is reflected in the desserts, which are mostly fried or baked pastries, biscuits and tarts. The tarts are often made with honey or filled with ricotta cheese that has been beaten to a cream with sugar. Considered too rich to serve at the end of a meal, except for special occasions, they are more often eaten

Previous pages: (clockwise from bottom left) *Sfogliatelle* (a typical Neapolitan pastry); *Cannoli alla Siciliana* (page 174); *Frutta di Martorana* (page 178); Fresh ricotta; *Fragoline di Bosco all'Arancio* (page 176)

as snacks between meals. Italian bars and *pasticcerie* are full of *babas*, *sfogliatelle*, *spumoni* and *crostate* to lift the spirits at any time of day.

Ice creams, sorbets and granitas are of a very high quality. The South, especially Sicily, is home to the most wonderful ice creams, which traditionally are made by artisans using only the best ingredients. Ice-cream making started with sorbets and granitas, reminiscent of the Arab custom of storing snow from Etna in purpose-built caves. This was then mixed with fruit juices to produce refreshing sorbets. Much later, with the advent of new technology, snow was replaced with milk and cream, giving birth to ice cream.

Sitting outside a café in summer and eating a lemon granita served in half a lemon or a *granita al caffe* made with very strong espresso epitomizes the way of life in most of the regions, where people spend time on the street and in the piazzas rather than at home so they can enjoy the wonderful weather.

RAVIOLO FRITTO AL MIELE DI FIOR D'ARANCIO
Fried Raviolo with Orange Blossom Honey

SERVES 4

4 pieces of pecorino cheese, cut into circles 10 cm (4 in) in diameter and 5 mm (¼ in) thick

Olive oil for deep-frying

120 ml (4 fl oz) orange blossom honey

FOR THE DOUGH

150 g (5 oz) *doppio zero* (00) flour (see page 14)

1 egg

1 egg yolk

A pinch of salt

1 tablespoon caster sugar

To do justice to the exceptionally good orange blossom honey from Pietro Pizzimenti in Calabria I borrowed a recipe from Sardinia because I thought the two would combine to produce perfection. The Sardinian raviolo called sabadas, *or* sebadas, *is usually flavoured with local honey but I find the Calabrese honey quite irresistible.*

METHOD

To make the dough, pile the flour up into a volcano shape on a work surface and make a large well in the centre. Put the egg, egg yolk, salt and sugar in the well and beat lightly with a fork. With your hands, gradually mix in the flour. When the mixture has formed a dough, knead it well with the palms of your hands for about 10 minutes, until it is very smooth and elastic. Cover and leave to rest for 20 minutes.

Bees native to this orange grove on Pietro Pizzimenti in Calabria produce delicious orange blossom honey

Roll out the dough until it is about 3 mm (¹/₈ in) thick. Cut out 8 rounds 15 cm (6 in) in diameter, re-rolling the trimmings as necessary. Put a piece of pecorino cheese in the centre of 4 of the rounds. Brush the edges of the dough rounds with water and cover with the remaining dough rounds, gently pressing the edges together to seal.

Heat plenty of olive oil in a pan and fry the ravioli for about 3–4 minutes, until brown and crisp on both sides. Put on individual serving plates, pour the honey over and serve immediately.

TORTA DI FAVE
Broad Bean Cake

SERVES 4–6

600 g (1 lb 5 oz) young broad beans (shelled weight)

6 eggs

300 g (11 oz) caster sugar, plus extra for sprinkling

6 tablespoons dried breadcrumbs

6 tablespoons extra virgin olive oil

Of all the culinary oddities, this Sardinian cake is one of the most peculiar. It must have been invented by a farmer with plenty of broad beans in his field. I tried it and it tastes better than it sounds. The freshness of the broad beans is paramount: they must be young and tender. However, I have tried it with blanched and peeled frozen ones, which worked well.

METHOD

Blanch the broad beans in boiling water for 1 minute and then drain. Slip them out of their skins.

Beat the eggs with the sugar until foamy and then stir in the beans and breadcrumbs. Heat the oil in a large, heavy-based frying pan. Pour in the mixture and cook gently until browned underneath, then carefully turn over and brown the other side. Sprinkle with more sugar and serve. It is good hot or cold.

CANNOLI ALLA SICILIANA
Sicilian Cannoli

MAKES 16

25g (1 oz) butter

25g (1 oz) caster sugar

1 egg

3½ tablespoons dry white wine

2 tablespoons vanilla sugar

A pinch of salt

150 g (5 oz) *doppio zero* (00) flour (see page 14)

Beaten egg for sealing the cannoli

Lard or vegetable oil for deep-frying

Icing sugar for dusting

FOR THE FILLING

500 g (1lb 2 oz) very fresh ricotta cheese

100 g (4 oz) caster sugar

1 tablespoon vanilla sugar

2 tablespoons orange flower water

50g (2 oz) mixed candied peel, finely chopped

50 g (2 oz) candied angelica, finely chopped

There's a little work to do if you want to eat one of the best Southern specialities. Every bar or pasticceria *in the South makes these pastries, which were originally the symbol of Sicily. They are eaten at any time as a pleasant little calorie shot to regenerate the powers!*

To shape the cannoli you will need some pieces of bamboo cane or metal tube, about 15 cm (6 in) long and 2 cm (¾ in) thick.

METHOD

To make the pastry, beat the butter and caster sugar together until light and creamy. Beat in the egg and then beat in the wine, vanilla sugar and salt. Mix in the flour and knead for 5–10 minutes, until smooth and elastic. Cover and leave in the fridge for at least 2 hours.

Roll out the dough until it is 2 mm (¹⁄₁₂ in) thick, then cut it into sixteen 12.5 cm (5 in) squares. Place a piece of bamboo cane or metal tube diagonally across each square of pastry and wrap 2 opposite corners around the cane. Seal with beaten egg. Make 3 or 4 at a time (this number will probably be dictated by the number of cannoli moulds you have).

Heat some lard or vegetable oil in a large deep pan – the fat must be deep enough to cover the cannoli completely. When it is very hot, carefully put in 3 or 4 cannoli and fry until golden brown – this will only take 1½–2 minutes. I find a long-pronged fork is the best implement for handling the cannoli in the

50 g (2 oz) glacé cherries, finely chopped

90g (3½ oz) plain chocolate, finely chopped

boiling fat. Place the cannoli on kitchen paper to drain. When they are completely cool, remove the moulds.

To make the filling, beat the ricotta cheese with a fork, then mix in the caster sugar, vanilla sugar and orange flower water. The ricotta should become creamier in consistency. Stir in the candied peel, angelica, glacé cherries and chocolate. Fill the cannoli with the ricotta mixture and arrange on a plate. Dust with icing sugar and serve cool, but do not refrigerate.

FICHI VANIGLIATI AL FORNO
Baked Figs

SERVES 4

12 large, ripe figs

12 tablespoons vanilla sugar (or use caster sugar and a few drops of vanilla extract)

Figs are eaten in all sorts of ways in Italy – fresh, dried, baked, etc. – but this simple recipe is particularly good. You could serve it with double cream. Italians, as a rule, don't but the choice is yours.

METHOD

Preheat the oven to 180°C, 350°F, Gas Mark 4.

Carefully peel the figs and arrange them close together on a baking tray. Sprinkle a spoonful of vanilla sugar over each one. Bake for 5 minutes and then place under a hot grill for 2–3 minutes. The figs will exude a lovely pinkish syrup and their tops should be covered with a crust of sugar. They can be served hot but are also wonderful eaten chilled.

FRAGOLINE DI BOSCO ALL'ARANCIO
Wild Strawberries with Orange

SERVES 4

400 g (14 oz) freshly picked wild strawberries

2 tablespoons caster sugar

Juice of 2 oranges, preferably blood oranges

A very simple dessert with an excellent combination of ingredients. If you cannot get wild strawberries, cultivated ones will do.

METHOD

If using cultivated strawberries, cut up any large ones. Put the strawberries in a bowl with the sugar and mix well, then leave to stand for an hour or two. Divide between individual dishes and pour the orange juice over just before serving.

Choosing wild strawberries in Palermo

PESCHE FRITTE
Fried Peaches

SERVES 8

250 g (9 oz) caster sugar

300 g (11 oz) ricotta cheese

½ teaspoon cinnamon

3 hard-boiled egg yolks

8 ripe peaches

Flour for dusting

1 egg, beaten

Dried breadcrumbs for coating

Olive oil for deep-frying

This recipe is my invention, using Southen ingredients in a Northern way. The result is delicious.

METHOD

Put the sugar, ricotta, cinnamon and hard-boiled egg yolks in a bowl and mix together well, then pass through a sieve. (Alternatively you can whizz everything together in a food processor.) Chill for 2 hours, until firm.

Cut the peaches in half, then twist and remove the stone carefully with a sharp knife. Take a small scoop and remove a little of the flesh from the centre. Mix the scooped-out flesh with the ricotta mixture and then fill the peach halves with this. Dust the peaches in flour, then coat with beaten egg and finally coat with dried breadcrumbs.

Heat the olive oil and deep-fry the peaches for a few seconds, until golden brown. They can be served hot or cold, with *Vino Cotto* (see page 189) if liked.

FRUTTA DI MARTORANA
Marzipan Fruits

MAKES ABOUT 1 kg (2¼ lb)

500 g (1 lb 2 oz) almonds

500 g (1 lb 2 oz) caster sugar

225 g (7½ fl oz) water

1 sachet of vanilla powder, or a few drops of vanilla extract

A selection of food colourings

This is a basic recipe for a traditional Sicilian speciality, named after the convent of Martorana where it was invented. In Sicily the marzipan is shaped into all sorts of fruit, using special moulds, then coloured. You can try using your hands to make your own shapes.

To prepare the marzipan, also known as pasta reale, buy ready-ground almonds or grind your own, following the instructions in the recipe.

METHOD

Simmer the almonds in a large pan of boiling water for a couple of minutes, then drain and peel. Leave to dry, then grind them as finely as possible in a food processor.

Put the sugar, water and vanilla in a large pan and stir over a medium heat until the sugar has completely dissolved. Bring to the boil, add the ground almonds and stir constantly for about 5 minutes, until the mixture comes away from the sides of the pan. Pour on to a work surface and leave to cool slightly, then knead for a few minutes. It is now ready to shape as you like and paint with food colouring. Use your artistic sense to mix the colours!

Store the marzipan shapes in an airtight container. They keep well, as the marzipan does not contain eggs.

LA COTOGNATA DI ANTONIO
Antonio's Quince Paste

1.5 kg (3¼ lb) ripe quinces,
washed, cored and chopped
Caster sugar
Sugar crystals for dusting

Antonio Piceci, food writer and chef at the Barbablu restaurant in Lecce, gave me this recipe, which I like very much for its simplicity. I love quinces anyway!

METHOD

Put the quinces in a pan, pour in a glass of water, then cover and cook gently for 30–45 minutes until they disintegrate. Pass through a sieve to obtain a smooth purée. Weigh the purée, then weigh out an equal amount of caster sugar. Put the sugar in a clean pan with a small glass of water, heat gently until dissolved, then bring to the boil and boil until pale brown. Remove from the heat. Put the quince purée in a separate pan and stir over a medium heat until the excess moisture has evaporated. Add the hot sugar syrup and stir very well for a few minutes.

Spread the paste in a lightly oiled baking tray in a layer about 1 cm (½ in) thick. Leave to cool and set, then cut into cubes and dust with sugar crystals. Store in an airtight tin. It is delicious served with coffee.

Following pages (from left): *Fichi Vanigliati al Forno* (page 175); *Pesche Fritte* (page 177) served with *Vino Cotto* (page 189)

STRUFFOLI DI NAPOLI
Neapolitan Struffoli

SERVES 10

5 medium eggs

3 tablespoons granulated
   sugar

500 g (1 lb 2 oz) *doppio zero*
   (00) flour (see page 14)

Grated rind of 1 orange

Grated rind of 1 lemon

1 tablespoon pure alcohol (if
   not available, use strong
   vodka)

A pinch of salt

Olive oil or lard for deep-
   frying

FOR THE CARAMEL

250 g (9 oz) honey

100 g (4 oz) caster sugar

2 tablespoons water

FOR DECORATION

25 g (1 oz) small sugar silver
   balls

50 g (2 oz) *cedro* (see page
   21), cut into small cubes

Rind of 1 tangerine, cut into
   very thin strips

The origin of this classic recipe is the fruit of the imagination of the once poor people of Naples who make this dessert with fried pastry pellets substituting the more expensive hazelnuts. The recipe has a touch of Arabic influence to it due to frying in oil and flavouring with honey.

METHOD

To make the dough, beat the eggs lightly with the sugar, then mix in the flour, orange and lemon zest, alcohol and salt. Knead well for 3–4 minutes, then shape into a ball. Cover and leave to rest for 2 hours in a cool place.

Take a little bit of dough at a time and roll with your hand into sausage shapes about 1 cm (½ inch) thick. Cut into pieces 1 cm (½ inch) long. It is quite laborious rolling out the dough and will take you some time.

Heat the oil or lard in a pan so that it is 2.5 cm (1 in) deep. Fry the struffoli, quite a few at a time, in the hot oil until lightly browned, then remove and drain on kitchen paper.

To make the caramel, gently heat the honey, sugar and water in a large pan until the sugar has dissolved. Add the *struffoli* and stir carefully until they are all coated with the caramel. Arrange on a plate. Decorate with silver balls (not too many), *cedro* and tangerine rind, then leave to cool. They will taste delicious!

TORTA CAPRESE DI MANDORLE
Capri Almond and Chocolate Cake

MAKES A 25 cm (10 in) CAKE

200 g (7 oz) bitter chocolate

200 g (7 oz) butter, softened

6 eggs, separated

200 g (7 oz) caster sugar

50 g (2 oz) *doppio zero* (00) flour (see page 14)

½ teaspoon baking powder

300 g (11 oz) blanched almonds, finely chopped

2 tablespoons Strega liqueur

Icing sugar for dusting

Amongst all the magnificent Southern cakes and tarts, the torta Caprese *is notable for the splendid result that is obtained with relatively little effort. 'A piece of cake,' you might say.*

METHOD

Preheat the oven to 180°C, 350°F, Gas Mark 4.

Break up the chocolate, put it in a pan with the butter and melt over a low heat. Leave to cool.

Beat the egg yolks with the sugar until thick and pale, then fold in the flour and baking powder. Carefully fold in the chocolate mixture, almonds and Strega. In a separate bowl, beat the egg whites until stiff and then gently fold them into the mixture. Pour into a buttered shallow 25 cm (10 in) cake tin and bake for 30 minutes, until well risen. If you test it with a skewer, the cake should still be a little moist in the centre. Turn out on to a wire rack and leave to cool, then dust with icing sugar.

Following pages (from left):

Torta Caprese di Mandorle (above);

Struffoli di Napoli (page 182)

MELANZANE E CIOCCOLATO
Chocolate Aubergines

SERVES 6

1 large aubergine, weighing about 300 g (11 oz)

2 tablespoons plain flour

4 eggs, beaten

Olive oil for frying

FOR THE FILLING

50 g (2 oz) fresh breadcrumbs, soaked in 2 tablespoons of milk

50 g (2 oz) pine kernels, toasted and finely chopped

100 g (4 oz) candied peel, finely chopped

25 g (1 oz) walnuts, toasted and finely chopped

½ teaspoon cinnamon

1 tablespoon Strega liqueur or Marsala (or some other sweet liqueur)

FOR THE CHOCOLATE SAUCE

120 ml (4 fl oz) double cream

2 tablespoons Strega liqueur

200 g (7 oz) plain chocolate

2 teaspoons cocoa powder

This intriguing recipe comes from the Amalfi coast and is very popular in the towns of Positano, Minori and Ravello. This version is from the family of Gennaro Contaldo, my valuable assistant, who comes from Minori.

METHOD

Mix all the ingredients for the filling together and set aside.

To make the chocolate sauce, put all the ingredients in a bowl set over a pan of barely simmering water and leave until the chocolate begins to melt. Remove from the pan of water and stir until the chocolate has melted and the sauce is smooth.

Slice the aubergine very thinly lengthways, about 2 mm ½ in thick. (Discard the slices at both ends which will be skin only.) You should end up with 12 slices. Take each slice and coat in the flour, shaking off the excess. Dip into the beaten egg, draining off the excess egg. Heat a pan of oil and fry the aubergine slices over a gentle heat until golden on both sides. Remove and dry on kitchen paper, trying to blot off as much oil as possible.

Take an aubergine slice and spread some of the filling over it, then top with another aubergine slice, pressing hard with your hand so that the filling is tightly sealed. Dip the aubergine 'sandwich' into the remaining egg, shaking off any excess, and fry briefly in the hot oil again until both sides are golden. Remove from the oil and drain thoroughly on kitchen paper. Coat in the chocolate sauce, place on a plate and serve. If you have any extra chocolate sauce, you can pour it over the top. Delicious!

RICOTTA ALLO ZUCCHERO
Sugared Ricotta

SERVES 4

500 g (1 lb 2 oz) very fresh ricotta

120 g (4½ oz) caster sugar

A pinch of cinnamon

The best ricotta is made from sheep's milk and should be eaten raw when very, very fresh, just dusted with sugar. This is the dessert we children used to have when our mother was busy.

METHOD

Divide the ricotta between 4 serving plates and sprinkle with the sugar and cinnamon.

SGROPPINO
Special Lemon Sorbet

SERVES 4

6 scoops of lemon ice cream

100 ml (3½ fl oz) iced vodka

2 glasses of good prosecco or champagne

Here is a suggestion for a dish that makes a perfect end to a meal or, if you like, a break during a multi-course dinner. At La Taverna restaurant in Palau, Sardinia, we finished our excellent fish meal with this sorbet when we were filming there.

METHOD

For the best results you should use a blender and make sure all the ingredients are very cold, including the glasses in which they are to be served. Put all the ingredients into the blender and blend until you get a firm and frothy consistency. Serve immediately in glasses, with spoons.

ZABAGLIONE ALLA PERA
Pear Zabaglione

SERVES 4

12 free range egg yolks

4 tablespoons caster sugar

120 ml (4 fl oz) Poire William liqueur

Experimenting with zabaglione, I discovered that a great variety of flavours could be achieved by substituting different liquids for the traditional Marsala. I had the most success with Poire William liqueur but Cointreau and blackberry and raspberry liqueurs also worked well. Using the egg yolks as a vehicle for the flavouring, it's up to you to discover new combinations – perhaps even trying fresh fruit juices such as passion fruit.

METHOD

Put the egg yolks and sugar in a large bowl, preferably a copper one, and whisk until thick and pale. Add the liqueur and mix well. Set the bowl over a pan of barely simmering water, making sure the water is not touching the base of the bowl, and whisk constantly until the mixture becomes a thick foam. Pour into glasses and serve immediately, accompanied by little biscuits such as amarétti if liked.

VINO COTTO
Reduced Wine Syrup

MAKES 250 ml (8 fl oz)

500 ml (17 fl oz) red wine,
preferably a strong one

200 g (7 oz) granulated sugar

Anyone brought up in the South of Italy will remember vino cotto – *a dense, treacly liquid made by boiling down red grape must. In summer it is diluted with water to make a refreshing drink, while in winter it can be poured on to a snowball, which is then sucked as a sort of primitive sorbet. It is also often used in biscuits and cakes or to flavour all sorts of desserts and fruit salads.*

As red grape must is not easy to obtain, I have simply boiled red wine in this recipe, resulting in a different flavour from the original but heavenly nevertheless. Most of the alcohol evaporates when the wine is boiled so it is quite suitable for children. When it was photographed for this book with Pesche Fritte *(see page 177), the photographer tasted it and said, 'This is food for lovers.'*

METHOD

Put the wine and sugar in a heavy-based pan over a moderate heat and heat until the sugar has dissolved. Boil until the mixture has reduced by almost two-thirds to 250 ml (8 fl oz). Leave to cool, then bottle and store in the fridge.

INDEX